How To Keep Your Doctor Happy

How To Keep Your Doctor Happy

John Larkin

W F HOWES LTD

This large print edition published in 2013 by
W F Howes Ltd
Unit 4, Rearsby Business Park, Gaddesby Lane,
Rearsby, Leicester LE7 4YH

1 3 5 7 9 10 8 6 4 2

First published in the United Kingdom in 2012
by Sandstone Press Ltd

Copyright © John Larkin, 2012

The right of John Larkin to be identified as
the author of this work has been asserted by him
in accordance with the Copyright, Designs and
Patents Act, 1988.

All rights reserved

A CIP catalogue record for this book is available
from the British Library

ISBN 978 1 47122 561 1

Typeset by Palimpsest Book Production Limited,
Falkirk, Stirlingshire

Printed and bound in Great Britain
by TJ International Ltd, Padstow, Cornwall

MIX
Paper from
responsible sources
FSC
www.fsc.org   FSC® C013056

For Malachy

CONTENTS

INTRODUCTION 1
SPOUSES, FAMILY AND STRANGERS 6
THE CONSULTATION 20
CIGARETTES & ALCOHOL . . .
(and CALORIES) 40
KNOW YOUR ENEMY 50
SURGICAL SPECIALTIES 60
MEDICAL SPECIALTIES 71
STUDENTS 77
GIFTS 85
CLOTHES 90
GETTING YOUR OWN BACK 95
DON'T MENTION THE WARD –
THINGS NOT TO SAY IN THE
CONSULTING ROOM 110
DON'T MUNCH IN THE WARD –
THINGS NOT TO DO IN THE
CONSULTING ROOM 128
PHRASES THAT SAY YOU'RE
MAKING IT UP 137
SYMPTOMS NOT WORTH
MENTIONING AS EVERYBODY
GETS THEM 149

TEN DON'TS AND DOS FOR
MEDICAL IN-PATIENTS   153
PRIVATE MEDICINE   161
ALTERNATIVE MEDICINE   174
MAL'S PRACTICE – THE GP
PERSPECTIVE   185
GLOSSARY   207

PREFACE

There are two sorts of books that doctors write for patients.

The first sort is set in the garden of touchy-feeliness, where medics and patients all get on swimmingly. It is full of self-help hints on how to look after your toe-nails, gums or prostate (requiring surprisingly similar techniques), but also advises precisely when to invoke the help of your ever-friendly GP.

The second sort acknowledges that the doctor-patient relationship is not always a bed of roses, but realises that any problem will without exception be the fault of the doctor. The basic premise is that all-doctors-are-evil, and are singlehandedly responsible for each and every breakdown in communication. A second-sort book will be replete with stories of doctors being arrogant, stupid, and other varieties of wrong. While aimed at the general populace, it will be liberally sprinkled with advice for medics as to how they could better relate to their flock. Not for a moment does it consider the possibility that the patient 'could do better'.

This is the third sort.

Leabharlanna Poibli Chathair Bhaile Átha Cliath
Dublin City Public Libraries

INTRODUCTION

What about that title? *How to keep Your Doctor Happy*. Not something you'll normally worry about, and no doubt two major questions spring to mind:

One: what exactly do I mean by keeping your doctor happy? Two: why would you want to do that?

OK. By keeping your doctor happy we're not talking about getting him a rise in salary, or spanking new premises, or wall-to-wall electrodiagnostic devices. Because none of that is at all important. You ask any person in any job dealing with the public what pleases or upsets them most and they'll all say the same thing. The punters. Being a teacher is child's play, provided the little bandits aren't throwing things at you, or their parents pounding your desk demanding to know why their little Einstein keeps failing exams (and it doesn't help to point out that so did Albert). A waiter's lot is a happy one until the guy who sent back the over-cooked steak, undercooked lettuce, and the wine that didn't go with his chewing gum finds he's left his credit card in Barcelona. Even

1

a taxi-driver can keep a smile on his face until somebody throws up in the back seat. The Public is Enemy No 1.

In fact, it's not even about keeping your doctor happy, it's about *not driving your doctor up the wall*.

Simple.

Knowing the things that annoy doctors most and trying to avoid them. To help us, we'll learn to see a few things from the doctor's point of view. Give it a try. By seeing it from their side, we'll spot the often normal and sensible things that people do which irritate doctors – just because it's not what the doctor wants them to do – and avoid them. All the best books about child psychology take this approach; avoid tantrums by avoiding the situations which set off tantrums. It should be no major jump to another group that likes the world to revolve round them. Some general medical knowledge might also help, since it's easier to have what the doctor will regard as a fruitful conversation if you have an idea what he's rambling on about – but NOT TOO MUCH. That would be a rookie mistake. We want to sound as if we understand what he's telling us, but not as if we know more about it than he does. So, as I take you through the titbits of advice in this little book, with a minimum of effort you should also pick up some knowledge of doctors and matters medical – but not too much . . . he wouldn't like that . . .

Just a mo.

What's all this '*he* wouldn't like that' stuff? Not

all doctors are male. In fact, most doctors these days are female. Are we going to go through this book pretending all doctors are male? Isn't that sexist?

Well . . . yes, and . . . (hopefully) no.

Let's look at the options.

1 We do that whole 'he/she thought he'd/she'd lost his/her . . .' sort of thing. Gets tedious.
2 We use 'they' as a singular noun. Often awkward, and sometimes tempts me to invent words. 'Then the doctor did the same thing themself . . .'
3 We use 'he' sometimes, 'she' others. Might work. Can be confusing. Occasionally jars . . . and why exactly 'she' this time and 'he' last time?
4 Use 'she' all the time.

Statistically correct.

But I'm going to ignore that and use 'he' every time unless there's a very good reason not to. Because those statistically female doctors are still *mainly* youngsters. This book isn't about keeping them happy. It's the seniors you need to worry about – and they're usually males . . . wrinkled old curmudgeonly types. People like me! Perhaps not surprisingly, this book's about keeping people like me happy . . .

★　　★　　★

. . . which brings us to question two. Why would you want to do that? Why bother? Why keep any doctor happy? They are invariably smug, insensitive, opinionated people paid far more than you are for a job that doesn't appear particularly onerous.

I could trot out the old arguments: that he's devoted countless hours to meticulous study during years of training, sacrificing time and energy both then and now for his patients, and that the job itself while physically undemanding does entail oodles of mental pressure. However, you are unlikely to swallow a word of that. In these days of GPs' 'opting out' of night-cover and hospital doctors in perpetual training-mode until they begin winding down for retirement, I'm not that convinced myself. It obviously isn't that bad a job, and the stresses and strains certainly lack obvious danger-to-self. I'd rather be a doctor than a coal-miner.[1]

But I'm not making a case that they *deserve* to be kept happy.

Instead, I'll state two simple facts, and leave you to draw your own conclusion:

---

[1] Though it does raise hackles when TV commentators go on about the monumental stress professional sportsmen are under. Take the golfer's 'pressure putt'. Even if he misses a tiddler that your granny would slot home, they'll still let him play next week. Do the equivalent in an operating theatre and they take away your clubs.

1 Your doctor is the person you tell your secrets to, the person who decides what's wrong with you, what invasive investigations you need, and what potentially dangerous drugs you will be given.

2 Back where I come from, people were always wary of upsetting Italian waiters ... in case they spat in your cappuccino ...

SPOUSES, FAMILY, FRIENDS AND STRANGERS

The first thing you have to think about when going to see your doctor is 'who should I take with me?' And the undeniably correct answer is . . . 'nobody', or more precisely: 'For God's sake, NOBODY! ARE YOU CRAZY?? LEAVE THEM ALL AT HOME!!!'

It is a fact universally unacknowledged that any doctor is far from happy with the current trend for patients to bring a 'companion' (mother, best friend, best friend's mother, best friend's mother's best friend . . .) into the consulting room.

Why is this?

Surely a companion can be a comfort in trying times, an aidememoire for the patient's history telling, a calm observer who can help the patient afterwards remember all the things the doctor talked about?

Maybe.

But essentially the doctor views the primary role of all companions as that of TROUBLEMAKER – eager to pounce on any errors or deficiencies in his interview or examination technique. And it's tricky for any of us to do our job with someone looking over our shoulder. Think about it. Would you really want the garage mechanic to try to fix your cherished Lamborghini while your wife constantly prods him with a stick, saying . . . *whatye doin' now? . . . don't bother with that, it's this bit that's causing the trouble . . . what have you found so far? . . . You'd better fix this right, it's the only one we've got . . .*

And don't think I'm putting you off bringing a companion purely for the doctor's benefit. Even from the patient's point of view, having a companion ain't all it's cracked up to be. Let's look at the possibilities.

Spouse

Arguably the worst person to bring with you. They're forever putting in their tuppenceworth at any non-opportune moment:

Patient:	*Well, the pains started last Friday, Doctor. They –*
Spouse:	*No it wasn't. You had them before that.*
Patient:	*No I didn't. I . . .*
Spouse:	*You had them on the way back from Aunt Jemima's . . .*
Patient:	*Aunt Jemima's* **was** *Friday*
Spouse:	*Your other Aunt Jemima's . . . sorry about this, Doctor, she's a bit demented at times . . .*
Patient:	*Me? Demented? It's you that . . .*

7

Once the doctor spots discord in the ranks, he'll jump on the chance to disbelieve everything you say. To his delight, the potential troublemaker now becomes his ally, and you'll find them sharing winks, nods and 'knowing expressions' while silently mouthing 'woman's troubles . . .' or '. . . men, huh!' – whichever is appropriate.

At a more serious level, there's lots of things that you really don't want to discuss in front of your partner. And when you see a doctor, you never know where the conversation is going to end up. A young man with a suddenly swollen knee may not realise that this could be a reactive arthritis following a urinary tract infection, and that any doctor worth his salt will want to ask him if he's had any . . . 'new partners' recently. Sending the wife out for coffee might cover your tracks, but better if you don't bring her in the first place – then you won't have to send her out for coffee every subsequent visit to make out this is normal practice.

Sister

Arguably the worst person to bring with you.

Sisters, in all aspects of life, are a bristling bag of paradoxical emotions. They want the best for their sister . . . but not quite as good a best as they want for themselves. Looks, dresses, houses, husbands . . . it goes for health too. So they're desperate to show sis how much they care, and make sure the doctor does everything in their power to help. But all this time they'll make damned sure the doctor isn't neglecting *them*. Initially this is in relation to the patient. They'll insist their diagnostic musings get some airing. Then they'll throw in the occasional symptom of their own to encourage you to take their experienced opinions seriously, a bit more detail to suggest you now take their *symptoms* seriously, a bit further-more for 'family background', until it eventually becomes clear that *their* needs eclipse those of the patient, who can be put on the back-burner whilst the doctor takes care of *them*.

And if the doctor misjudges exactly how to deal with the question of which sister is older than the other, or (worse) *looks* older . . .

Brothers

Would be arguably the worst . . . except . . . I don't remember anyone ever bringing their brother.

Parents

Arguably the worst people to bring with you.

Of course, the whole companion-being-a-good-thing thing started with the concept of parents accompanying toddlers to see the doctor – entirely proper (somebody's got to hold them down) – but teenagers arriving with a parent makes no sense at all. Smoking, drinking, drugs, sexual habits and orientation (not always the same) are all things that the doctor might want to know about before he can make a wild guess (oops, just slipped out) at what's wrong. And it's no good planning to bring a parent along only when all your secrets won't be relevant because a) you don't know when that is (you might have a swollen knee!) and b) if you try that tactic, then whenever you do go to the doctor on your own, they're gonna be *so* suspicious . . .

The above refers to teenagers, and if you're a fully-grown forty-something, why oh why oh why would you even think about bringing a parent along? ('cos some of them do).

Children

Arguably the worst people to bring along.

We are not, of course, talking about young children or toddlers who clamber over the chairs and rummage around in the drawers full of syringes and needles. They're good fun. Certainly a welcome distraction, and often an opportunity for the doctor to bond with the patient by showing his[1] human side. A friendly but firm 'that's brilliant, Joseph;

[1] I considered breaking my rule here, and writing 'his/her'. However, in this scenario it seems appropriate to keep '*his* human side' as it's generally accepted that in order to survive all female doctors have been obliged to sell theirs off at an early stage.

now how about throwing the needles into this bucket? More of a challenge than Julie's pram . . .' can work wonders, as can gently cajoling away the tears and fears as his mother is clearly being assaulted by a stranger (oddly, most children will observe impassively whilst needles are jabbed into mum's arm, but panic the moment she lies down to have her tummy examined. I think there's an innate fear of lying-down-means-going-to-die in all our psyches – indeed I often find myself propping patients up further in bed when examining them, as seeing them lying flat makes *me* worried).

No.

It's the adult children that are the problem. In fact, from your doctor's perspective, there's no 'arguably' about it. In fact again, it's time for my first Top Tip

Top Tip No 1
Do not bring any of your grown-up children with you when you go to see the doctor.

The worst people to accompany you on your visit to the doctor are grown-up children.

There. I've said it. It's official. Daughters worse than sons. Two daughters worse than one. Canadian daughters worst. This hierarchy of badness is entirely explained by the reason they are there. Everyone (including naïve medics who take their prompt from what they read in the newspapers) assumes it's because they love their mother, are worried about her, want the best for her and want to make sure that everything possible is done for her.

But that's bollocks.

Each and every daughter is there for one reason. To show their mother that they love her more than the other daughter does.

To the doctor, this is an absolute nightmare. The aforementioned spouse-companion's interjections were often unhelpful, but usually well-meaning. Here they are replaced by interruptions with one goal in mind. Show *how much you care.* And not just for the mother's benefit. It doesn't stop if she's out of the room, or on the other side of the planet (we'll get to the Canada thing). The sister has to prove to the other sister how much she loves mum; she has to prove to the doctor how much she loves mum; basically she has to prove to herself . . .

So the doctor has to put up with lurid accentuations of just how painful someone else's pains are, how stiff someone else's stiffness is, and big lists of things that someone else's weakness makes them unable to do . . . 'it's really bad first thing in the morning when she's trying to put up a curtain rail'. All of the doctor's questions will be wrong (bouncing between pointless and offensive), all of his investigations will have been done already, and – the worst – it will soon become clear why the doctor is not getting to the bottom of things . . . *he does not care enough.*

This is normally highlighted with the admonition, 'but Doctor, you've got to remember. She might be just another patient to you, but it's my *mother* we're talking about.' Many doctors take exception to this accusation that they care less than the relative does, some even claiming 'of course I do.' But clearly this is nonsense. The truth has to be that the doctor *does not* care about the patient as much as her daughter does. How could he? He has twenty other patients in the ward to worry about, hundreds more attending his clinic, and . . . he probably has *his* mother to worry about. He cannot spend all day, as the daughter is forced to, caring about her mother. All he can do is care *for* her as best as he can.

Still we doctors seem to find such non-accusations upsetting. Perhaps our real resentment is the subtext that we are consciously not trying hard enough . . . like the universal suspicion that the garage mechanic is deliberately failing to find the real fault so that he can keep charging us for all that other stuff he is doing.[2] My dream is one

---

[2] Clearly unfair on garage mechanics, who will no more make up diagnoses than I do. But I like using the analogy of garage mechanic or plumber to explore some relationships between patients and doctors. At least it would make sense for a garage mechanic to deliberately avoid the correct diagnosis, since he can charge for interim procedures. I don't see why a doctor would do so (except in the private sector, but we'll get to that).

day to tell the whingeing daughter the honest truth – that it cuts both ways. 'We'll make a deal. I'll remember she's your mother, you remember she *isn't* mine.' But I'm scared. Maybe the next time it's over the 'phone. Long distance. Maybe the next time it's a Canadian daughter . . .

Oh, all right then . . .

All doctors will tell you that Canadian daughters are the worst. They know everything. They question everything. No matter what's wrong with their mother, it would all have been sorted out by now if she was in Canada. All the tests would have been done within twenty-four hours of the first symptom (in a good hospital, they'd have it wrapped up in the twenty-four hours before), diagnosis made, and treatment instituted. Why Canadian daughters in particular? I reject my colleagues' suggestions that patients are charged 'piecemeal' for investigations and treatments in that country, and the doctors are rushing to fit in as many tests and remedies as possible quick before the patient spontaneously recovers. Surely that's too cynical? Canadians in general seem a reasonable bunch (suddenly realise . . . am not immediately in possession of any evidence to back that up) but as people-you-would-like-to-see-turn-up-accompanying-patients, they come bottom of the list. Fortunately most remain in Canada (it's so nice out there), and contact is mainly via protracted phone calls when they will insist that their mother has never looked so pale. Maybe they feel guilty about being miles away when their mother needs them, or that they need to make that extra effort vs. stay-at-home-sis who is in pole position in the *who loves mum most?* contest. But it is an unexplained fact that (in my experience at least) our friends from the Antipodes, South Africa or even the USA never seem to achieve the same levels of in-your-faceness.

Sons don't appear so often at consultations. But if one does, that's a warning-sign with more sinister implications for the doc. They're so much more into litigation . . .

Friends

Now the argument's settled, clearly not the worst people to bring along with you – but arguably the most bizarre. I mean . . . why? Bringing a 'friend' along induces the doctor's sub-cortex to dally with three possibilities.

1 The 'friend' is, in fact, a partner. Be this hetero- or non-hetero-, it makes no difference to the doctor ethically or morally but might put their diagnostications down the wrong path on a subliminal assumption that the diagnosis will somehow be related to that. Medicine is one big *Whodunnit*, and if in *Midsummer Murders* the 'friend' turns out to be a sexual partner . . . it's always for a reason.

2 The friend is medical or paramedical and is there to supply insight for both the patient and the doctor into what the other one is trying to say. This does raise my apprehensions – mainly that my standard slack approach will not go unremarked upon. Paradoxically, the main problem is that attempts to switch your standard relaxed approach into something else that you think will better impress the onlooker can lead to mistakes. However, most doctors are not fazed by the medical friend. Certainly much less so than . . .

3 The friend is someone who has been 'done over' by a doctor in the past (failed to spot diagnosis, failed to prescribe correct treatment, countersigned the uglier passport photo . . .) and is here to make sure it doesn't happen to his/her pal. This 'friend' is by far the most unrewarding from the doctor's point of view, and probably also from the patient's.

Interpreter

The one person you should bring along to a consultation is an interpreter. If, of course, this is appropriate. If you were born and brought up in Glasgow and your doctor is in Glasgow, then I'm not suggesting you bring your sister Anne-Marie with her PhD in French and Italian because she works in Brussels for the European Union. In fact, dragging in a family member who speaks the doctor's language a bit better than you is no good in any case, even when an interpreter is required.

You want a proper interpreter.

Despite the fact that we use the word 'interpreter' in preference to 'translator', a proper interpreter does not make the mistake of interpreting when he/she should simply translate. So a proper interpreter will tell the doctor everything the patient says and tell the patient everything the doctor says. The amateur interpreter eschews this approach. The doctor asks 'where's it sore?', the patient utters three words, pointing to her shoulder, and the helpful son-in-law goes into a long spiel about the terrible pains his mother-in-law is suffering in her back and legs which is worst in the afternoons, but again in the mornings, particularly when she's playing Frisbee. The 'family interpreter' will also pick and choose what bits he thinks worth translating, in both directions:

| Doctor | . . . *And I think you should lose some weight. Stop eating all those chips and cream cakes you were telling me about – and cheese, cheese is a killer-way of getting huge amounts of calories into you . . . and cut down to no more than two bottles of lemonade every morning. Eat more vegetables. Less fat and cream in your cooking. Exercise* |

	is good too. Walking, swimming, Yoga and Tai Chi – moves the muscles but doesn't ask the joints to do anything too fast . . .
Son-in-law	*Blah de blah blah*
Mother-in-law	*Na blah blah de blah*
Son-in-law	*She says it's no good, she can't swim*

Proper interpreters just translate. They never embellish or take sides or defend or attack the patient.[3] So if you *are* seeing a doctor in Glasgow and you come from anywhere south of Hadrian's Wall, I'd bring one along. Just make sure they don't gang up with the doctor against you ('cos that's what I try to get them to do).

So . . . interpreters aside . . . bring nobody. That way you get back to what a consultation with your doctor should be. A private discussion between equals – with one trying to help the other with their

---

[3] Not entirely true. I saw one Algerian woman with official interpreter, and simply told her 'it might help to lose some weight.' As far as my patchy French tells me, this was translated as: 'See? That's three doctors, one-two-three (counting on fingers . . . un . . . deux . . . trois . . .) and they're all saying the same thing. Cardiologist, Chest doctor and now (vague wave in my direction) rheumatology quack. You've got to lose weight. You're much too fat – look at you! You eat cakes all the time. And that's the cause of all your problems. If you'd only . . .'

problems. No second-guessing re confidentiality, professional competence, or upsetting a third party.

No interruptions for irrelevancies or accusations.

No lawyers . . .

THE CONSULTATION

The Introduction

Any doctor worth his salt will introduce himself to you. You won't need to introduce yourself back, since he'll already have 2000 bits of paper or bytes of hard drive telling him exactly who you are. He should, however, casually check that you are indeed the person he is expecting, if only to make sure he doesn't do a rectal examination on the guy who's come to fix the curtain rails. Now.

You'd think this intro, be it in a GP's surgery or a hospital consulting-room, would be a simple affair. 'Hi, Mrs Smith, I'm Doctor Jones, have a seat.' And in the past, you'd be dead right. But not any more. Doctors – or more correctly, doctor-educators – have discovered 'people skills'. Not good news. The curricula of trendy medical schools now include umpteen hours of intensive tuition on 'communication skills' and 'speaking to the patient'[1]. This is why

---

[1] Not the same thing. Part of the skill of speaking to the patient is not to communicate too much.

any medical student worth his overdraft will now approach you as if he's learned English from a tourist phrase-book. 'Good Morning Mrs Smith, my name is Clarence. I'm twenty-one years of age and I am a Third Year medical student. I wonder if it would be all right with you for me to sit myself down here just now and ask you a few questions about your . . .' (by which time, depending on diagnosis, you'll have gone off for a coffee or into cardiac arrest). This now has official approval. I examined in the Finals of my own Medical School recently and had to donate a mark to each candidate who introduced themselves 'correctly' plus a further mark if they outlined 'the purpose of the consultation'. My suggestion that this should be zero unless they said 'so I can become a doctor and make lots of money' fell on unimaginatively deaf ears.

Raising the importance of communication and empathy is all very well, but I believe 'teaching' such things smacks of artificiality and insincerity. If you have to learn how to be friendly and sincere, how can that be sincere? The 'ick' factor is increased by a number of current fads. One is for the doctor to introduce himself to you while calling you by your first name. 'Hello, Jenny. Sit down.' Clearly, this is a great idea. It makes everything more informal and friendly.

Bollocks again.

First names are 'friendly' for a reason. You use them between friends. To use them outwith that scenario is false and presumptious. A reasonable analogy is the use of the 'polite' form of address in languages such as French where you *vouvoyer* a stranger until you become chummy enough for one of you to suggest you might now *tutoyer*. The only people you immediately *tutoyer* are children and . . . servants. To anyone else it's an insult, including 'garçons' whom you'd never now tuttoyer (or indeed, call 'garçon'). Why anyone decided that calling a 65-year-old man you've met thirty seconds earlier by his first name was a good idea is beyond me. *Who* could conceivably think that . . .

Nurses!

Nurses have always enjoyed a better Press than doctors. To the public, doctors are scumbags, while nurses are the caring profession (within the hospital community, of course, the opposite is known to be the case). For many years nurses have adopted this 'are you needing the toilet, James?' approach to all and sundry having the misfortune to reside in their ward – from poet to peasant to High Court Judge. So, it is probably an ill-advised attempt by doctors to 'be like nurses' and curry favour with the general populace that explains their decision to adopt one of the nursing profession's more irritating habits.

[Not their *most* irritating habit, mind you. More impressive is doing all of the above at the top of their voices. 'PHILLIP! ARE YOU STILL NOT FINISHED WITH THAT BED-PAN. ARE YOU NEEDING ANY HELP? YOU'LL HAVE TO HURRY-UP. YOUR WIFE LIZZY'S HERE!'

Nurses have a perfectly-honed inability to speak

quietly, and will talk to a person standing next to them as if they were at the other end of the ward. At least, that is the impression you get until you hear them communicating with someone at the other end of the ward. The problem escalates with someone at the other end of a 'phone, where no confidence at all is shown in Marconi or Bell and their outlandish claims on electronic methods of transferring sound over long distances. Clearly anyone as far away as Kirkintilloch needs to be screamed at.

This is an opportunity for 'bonding' with your consultant during his ward-round. Nurses will accompany him, ostensibly to help carry out this onerous task. In reality they cause maximum disruption, finding some excuse to bawl at the patient in the next bed to the one the consultant has reached at any particular point. This will be particularly loud bawling in order to be heard over the shouts of porters picking up patients for Xrays (organized by the nurses to coincide with said Ward Round) and the wheezing mathematical calculations of the biscuit-lady[2]. When he tries in

---

[2] The pecking-order of ward dynamics may surprise you. Biscuit-sellers come at the top. If I'm writing in case notes at the ward-round-trolley and the biscuit-trolley comes by, I stop to let them pass. If I'm seeing a patient, I stop to let them buy biscuits. Conversely, if the patient is buying biscuits when I reach them, I wait for the transaction to be completed before speaking to them.

vain with his fancy stethoscope to hear your heart sounds over the hubbub (happens to me all the time – bizarrely, my first instinct is to put my fingers in my ears), a subtle raise of an eyebrow at the nurses' incessant chatter will endear you to the doctor for the duration.]

Where was I? Yeah. Irritations (other than ridiculously long brackets). First-name terms for patients. The 'patient as underling' effect of this first-name usage was eventually recognised, and the practice acknowledged as one of those supposed 'pc' manoeuvres which is in reality patronising. But a remedy was found. Balance up the presumption. The doctor would introduce himself to the patient using *his* first name. 'Hello, Jenny. I'm Lawrence. Would you like to take off your clothes and . . .?'

Of course this makes things worse. Not only is there now a double presumption (you are now forced to *tutoyer* the doctor) but the relationship makes no sense to the patient, since in their experience the only people who introduce themselves by their first names are children or people who work in MacDonald's.

Telling Your Story

Once the informalities are out of the way, the doctor will invite you to tell your story. This is the bit where you get to give a fairly uninterrupted account of what's troubling you. As with everything else, the doctor-educators have a technical name for this, but I don't like technical names for simple things so I refuse to use it. All right, the word actually escapes me right at this moment, but I'll look it up and append it as a footnote[3].

As you start this account, be aware of Top Tip No 2.

Top Tip No 2
Do not tell the doctor the diagnosis.

Think about it.

Five years of University, then five years of Junior Doctor Training, three years of research, ten years of further honing his skills in dedicated service to the NHS (whenever his private patients are having their tea) . . . does he really want you to come in and just give him the diagnosis? You don't go into the local garage and say 'the timer-belt's gone in my Renault.' No. Instead, you describe how you were driving down the motorway (probably *not* mentioning that you were *on your way to see your auntie in Dover where she's been living for the last two years ever since she moved from Liverpool after the kids left home . . . etc . . .)* when suddenly the car went 'kbangphut!' and simply stopped. The garage mechanic smiles wryly (perhaps after asking one or two questions):

---

[3] Forgot.

25

'Ah! That'll be the timer-belt.'

And you say.

'Really?'

And he lets you know how much it'll cost to fix – which is actually quite a lot. He then rubs it in by adding that if you'd had it seen to the day before it would have cost thruppence. Now, this sort of encounter should be your plan even if you *do* know about timer-belts. Good outcomes. The mechanic's happy as he's diagnosed your problem and shown off his prowess; you're happy (as far as a guy with an exploded engine can be) since your own diagnosis has been independently confirmed – properly, without your pushing the mechanic in that direction. And, if your diagnosis were to be absolute tosh it's no major embarrassment, as you haven't blurted it out loud.

The same thing should happen when you see your doctor. Tell him what happened, and let *him* diagnose it. Why don't people do this?

Look at the alternative. You tell the doctor what you think the diagnosis is. Immediately he's in trouble. He's under pressure to come up with the same diagnosis as you. Otherwise you may take offence. Indeed, from a position of having all the diagnoses in the world to pick from, he's now reduced to a choice of two. *Your* diagnosis, or . . . *something else*. And he knows that deciding on *something else* could lead to confrontation. Even if we don't have depending on it your job, marriage or compensation claims, you've still got your street cred to worry about. ('Actually Mr Rooney, I don't think the football socks are causing the rash, it's your leg-waxing technique that's all wrong'). So keep things friendly, and keep him happy by avoiding any attempts at self-diagnosis.

Even more important is to avoid other people's diagnoses.

*'Yes, your brother-in-law may well have had exactly the same symptoms and the operation may equally well have been a complete success, but the fact remains, Mrs Smith, that you don't actually **have** a prostate . . .'*

What seem to you the 'same symptoms' might have differences to a doctor. The one time I did think my timer-belt had gone *pbangphut!*, the garage mechanic was pretty quick to diagnose that I'd actually run out of petrol.

Suggested diagnoses from relatives and friends with a medical bent are particularly unwelcome. Just because your cousin who's a Staff Nurse in *Ear Nose and Throat* thinks you've got rheumatoid arthritis doesn't mean that you have, as far as your doctor is concerned. And, perhaps surprisingly, the least welcome suggestion as to the diagnosis comes from . . . any other doctor! Again, think about it. 'I went to see the doctors in St Thomas's and they said it was ME' puts even more pressure on your new doctor to agree – unless he's a contrary beggar ('Not ME'), whereupon the self-imposed pressure to do the opposite can be equally disruptive. Now when the new doctor comes up with an alternative, either he or the previous doctor has to be . . . WRONG!

Which brings us to one of the big problems in doctor-patient relationships. While patients and newspapers (and patients in newspapers) persistently complain that doctors think they're always right, most doctors I know are perpetually worried that they're wrong. They think of all diagnoses as 'working diagnoses' which they treat appropriately for as long as things go well and nothing new crops up to dispute it. You might suspect a doctor is overconfident in his diagnosis when something you see as contrary to his viewpoint doesn't change his mind – but the number one reason your observation doesn't worry him is because it doesn't conflict with his thinking in the first place. You just think it does. (Actually number two reason. The first *is* his bloodymindedness, but I'm trying to make a point here).

But the 'lay-person' isn't interested in 'working diagnoses'. To them a diagnosis is always definite and definitive. If I tell someone 'I think this might have been a heart attack,' then to them it was a heart attack. When the results prove I am way off the mark, a) that is no surprise to me (or any of my cheeky colleagues) and b) it is also no surprise when the patient says 'but you said I'd had a heart attack.' Nor is it a shock to find months later that they've told every doctor in the world that they had a severe heart attack and the quack looking after them sent them home without any treatment . . . just a second, I'll get you his name . . .

Part of the fall-out of this misapprehension is the attitude; *how can two doctors disagree over what I've got? How can one doctor say one thing, and another say something entirely different?* We hear this all the time. Yet the answer is – *very easily!* For an analogy we must leave my favourite garage mechanic scenario. Diagnosing a tricky case is even less certain, less definite, and more of a judgement call than what's wrong with my car. It's more like picking man-of-the-match at the FA Cup Final. A number of 'diagnoses' can be dismissed, such as the guy who missed a sitter before giving away the penalty in extra time. Also anyone playing on the losing side unless they were rank outsiders. [Thus if ManU beat Arsenal 2–1, no-one in the Arsenal side could possibly have played better than everyone in the ManU team. However, if ManU beat Kettering Town 24–1, one of the Kettering players (either the goalie or the guy who scored) will certainly be the best player on the park.] Eventually three or four candidates will appear, and it's a judgment call. So Gary Lineker and Alan Hanson can come up with different answers even though they both watched the same match. And two doctors given the same patient's history and examination can come up with two different 'most likely' diagnoses. Similar to Hanson picking a defender and Lineker a forward, the doctors will often come up with diagnoses from their own specialty[4].

But the world doesn't accept this. So we're back to the problem.

If you give the doctor another doctor's diagnosis, then he knows that if he disagrees, you'll think one of them is wrong, and you'll panic (or claim to panic).

So.

Just tell the doctor what the symptoms are/were, what you yourself were feeling wrong, and let him/her get on with having a stab at what's causing it. No second guesses, no what other people thought it might be, no things that it reminded you of that you read about in last month's *Cosmo*.

Just *tell your story*.

Dead easy . . .

Depending on his style, the doctor will either let you finish this before asking specific questions, or will interrupt (partly for clarification but mainly to break the monotony) at various points. The doctor-educators of course recommend the first technique. Evidently they never actually have to take a clinical history – or alternatively are happy to doze off, listening to wandering diatribes (are thae guys no mad?) about the private lives of aunties in Dover. Either way, when the doctor does ask his

---

[4] Except for surgeons on call. As explained elsewhere they will make 45 separate medical diagnoses before coming up with a reluctant surgical counter.

specific questions, we come to the devilishly clever
TopTip No 3.

Top Tip No 3
Answer the question!

This advice might appear obvious, but it's a well-known fact among medics that patients will never answer the question you ask them. Patients' idea of an 'answer' can be classified into ten categories:

1 **A diagnosis**
   What were the pains like?
   Oh – they're just my arthritis.

2 **Redefining your question**
   How long are you stiff for in the morning?
   Until I get up and move about and get a bit more mobile.

3 **Guessing why it is you're asking the question and giving an answer that is only helpful if their guess is right.**
   When you were young, were you the sort of person who can touch their toes very easily?[5]
   I never played sports.

---

[5] A question re 'hypermobility' – over-lax ligaments that make you prone to arthritis, whether you were sporty or not.

Do you keep pigeons?
Yes, but none of them has got a cough.

Have you recently had any new sexual partners?
Yes, but I didn't kneel down . . .

Or the classic:

What were you doing when the chest pain started?
Nothing. (i.e. 'I wasn't running around playing football . . . that was what you wanted to know, wasn't it?' Every patient who ever had chest pain was doing nothing at the time. Not standing, or sitting, or eating or having sex with the next-door-neighbour . . . NOTHING!)

4 Accidentally evasive
Have you had any pregnancies?
I'm not married.
Any risk factors for HIV?
Just that I go to Africa frequently.
(. . . er . . . and don't or do have unprotected sex with every man/woman you meet?)

5 Vague
Doc:	*So what's been the problem?*
Patient:	*The jandees*
Doc:	*'The jandees?'*

Patient:	Aye, the jandees. The yellow jandees.
Doc:	And how long have you had it . . . them?
Patient:	Oh, for quite a wee while now.
Doc:	And how long's that?
Patient:	Oh, quite a while.
Doc:	But how long's 'quite a while'?
Patient:	Ages.
Doc:	But how long is 'ages'?
Patient:	Quite a while.
Doc:	But how long is that? Two days?
Patient:	Naw. More than two days.
Doc:	Two months?
Patient:	Naw. Not as much as two months.
Doc:	So . . . more than two days, less than two months . . . a month maybe?
Patient:	Aye – about that.
Doc:	So you've had them about a month?
Patient:	Had what?
Doc:	THE JANDEES!
Patient:	Aw the jandees . . . aye, they've been for quite a wee while now . . .[6]

6 Unlucky

And the last time you had the chest pain was . . .?

A year ago

And what were you doing at the time?

I was an architect.

---

[6] *Cynical Acumen*, Radcliffe 2005, P62.

7 Deliberately evasive

Obviously the most upsetting answer for the doctor. Of course, no reader of this book would ever indulge in genuine deception, so my general advice is 'Don't be coy' and is further elucidated under 'Cigarettes and Alcohol.'

8 Answer whose main function is the Avoidance of Any Answer that might suggest for a moment that this isn't the worst disease that anybody's ever suffered in the whole world

At what time of the day is the pain worst?
All day. It's sore right now.
But what time of the day is it worse, . . . the morning? . . . the afternoon? . . . night? . . .
The morning
For how long is it worse in the morning?
All day . . .

What's the pain like? . . . sharp? . . . dull? . . . burning? . . . throbbing? . . .
It's really bad.

Does the pain come and go or is . . . ?
It's there all the time
Does it ever change?
No, it's stayed exactly the same
Has it got any better since . . . ?
No – it's got worse

Top Tip No 4
Don't keep telling the doctor how sore the pain is. If he asks when it starts or when it stops or where it starts or what brings it on or what makes it better, that's because this helps tell him what's causing it. Don't just keep telling him that it's really bad. That doesn't ANSWER THE QUESTION.

9 Given with an eye on their Benefits form
When are the pains worst?
When I'm doing light housework. I'm unable to do light house-work.
. . . What exactly is 'light housework'?
. . . erm . . . er . . . Chopping potatoes . . . no! . . . peeling potatoes and chopping vegetables.

And the most common

10 Absolutely nothing to do with the question.
What did the pain feel like?
It was there all day.

Did you feel anything else wrong at the same time?
My brother had exactly the same thing.

This category is so common that most doctors

have learned to assume patients' answers will bear no relation to the question. They remain oblivious as consultations take on the characteristics of a *Two Ronnies* sketch. For example, on a post-receiving ward-round.

Doctor:	*How you doin'?*
Patient:	*What?*
D:	*How you getting on?*
P:	*Whit?*
D:	*. . . any problems? . . . pains? . . .*
P:	*Ah'm fine*
D:	*. . . so whatye doing in hospital?*
P:	*[A LOOK] I'm just fine.*
D:	*So, no pains anywhere? Or cough, spit?*
P:	*Ah've got pains in ma chest.*
D:	*Right! So when did they start?*
P:	*Ma sister panicked and she 'phoned the ambulance.*
D:	*So the pains were quite bad?*
P:	*They were in ma chest – ah told ye. And I wis coughin' up something terrible.*
D:	*What exactly were you coughing up?*
P:	*Aw it wis sometime yesterday afternoon. Ma spit was green.*
D:	*Has this happened before?*
P:	*The pain wis terrible – worst ah've ever had.*
D:	*What were you doing when they started?*

36

P:	*Ah wis coughing up thick green phlegm.*
D:	*But how could you have the coughing up before it all started?*
P:	*I keep getting it all the time.*
D:	*But what were you actually doing at the time?*
P:	*I wis a plumber . . .*

And so on . . .

Now – must make apologies here. On its own, the above sequence is neither point-full nor particularly entertaining. If we *were* doing a *Two Ronnies* sketch we would be manipulating the underlying concept to achieve much more hilarious sexual innuendo than achieved above (and it wouldn't depend on an unlikely sputum fetish). But the point is, show the above to any doctor out of context and he'll think it's a true account of a meeting with a patient. You'll have spotted it, but the fact that the patient is answering the question before last will not even occur to him. Honest. Go on. Find a doctor and try it.

So . . . tell your story just as it happened, with no interpretations or diagnoses. And don't get upset if the doctor interrupts to ask about some apparently irrelevant detail, or bring you back from your favourite entirely unrelated anecdote (assuming your auntie in Dover is not related) to the matter at hand.

Examination

At some stage during the consultation, the doctor will call time-out and may suggest he examine you. This will be dealt with in unhelpfully sporadic detail elsewhere. Just room here for a few pointers.

1 Relax. The doctor's done this millions of times.
2 There's no hurry. It's not worth losing buttons or tearing zips in an attempt to be instantaneously ready for a full examination, or instantaneously ready to go home. The doctor is not an irate husband coming up the garden path.
3 Don't take off all your clothes. Much less embarrassing for everyone if you take off less than required, rather than more. However . . .
4 . . . Always take off more clothes than he does.
5 Follow his suggested manoeuvres – breathe out . . . breathe in . . . hands up . . . knees bent – rather than the manoeuvre you think he is about to suggest. Among other things, ignoring this advice can occasionally cost someone an eye.
6 Tell him if anything causes pain or discomfort. This may pinpoint an important clinical sign . . . as well as

(if you're lucky) helping you avoid pain and discomfort.

7 Don't be embarrassed if you would like a chaperone. Ask for this at the beginning of the examination. If you start off without, then ask for one in the middle of the examination, the doctor will get all worried that he's done something to make you suddenly wary. A bit like the husband who's cheerfully helping the police with their inquiries about the wife's disappearance then suddenly stops . . . 'I think I'd like a lawyer.' The cops would have to assume they've stepped over the mark somewhere.

CIGARETTES AND ALCOHOL . . .
AND CALORIES

Cigarettes

*H*ow many cigarettes a day do you smoke?
How did you know I smoked?
Just a guess. [I can smell it for a start –
plus you cough all the time, your face is all wrinkled
and your otherwise grey hair is browny-yellow at the
front]
Pause . . .
So . . . how many?
I've cut it down
To how many?
Nothing like as many as I used to
So how many?
A packet lasts me . . . days . . .
Days?
Well, a day . . . maybe . . .
And how big a packet is that?
. . . I get them at the airport . . .

What is the point?
If you're supposed to be telling your doctor

everything he needs to know to make a diagnosis and help you, why is it that everyone gets so evasive when it comes to answering questions about their cigarette and alcohol intake? The doctor is forced to focus down on the tiniest little detail in every statement in order to get to the truth, like Macbeth and his witches 'that palter with us in a double sense'. My own personal true-life favourite was:

> *Do you smoke cigarettes?*
> *I used to smoke at one time.*
> *When did you stop?*
> *. . . Tuesday.*

Why? It really is upsetting the doctor for no reason. There's no more point in lying to your doctor about cigarettes than lying to your garage mechanic as to how long it's been since you checked your oil (Ooops – I do that. Probably because I don't want him to think I'm a useless tube who deserves having his car fall apart. And since I don't realise that he can probably surmise the truth by . . . checking the oil, I make up a story in an attempt to hold onto my road-cred. Aaaargh. Suddenly it all makes sense . . . however . . .)

Just tell him how many cigarettes you smoke per day and it'll all be over. Of course, conventional wisdom is for the doctor to multiply this answer by two to achieve something nearer the truth. You say twenty, he assumes forty. Now that most patients know this, I advise my juniors that the patient will have allowed for this doubling, so really they should multiply the proffered answer by four . . . shouldn't have told you that . . . Now I'll have to multiply by *eight*. So anybody admitting to more than four per day has to go down as a chain-smoker.

Alcohol

When it comes to alcohol, people get even more vague (though they refrain from claiming they 'don't inhale'). They might say they drink 'once a week' – not mentioning that this is non-stop Friday afternoon until Monday morning. Alternatively, they may say they have 'just a few pints at the week-end' – omitting to clarify that this is of vodka. Similar to the 'doubling' manoeuvre with cigarettes, the medical response is a Devil's dictionary of re-interpreting vocabulary. And whilst they may be cheeky, I think you should be aware of their presumptions:

A couple is a random number never less than four. Why is this? Ask anybody in the street – recently married or not – just how many there are in 'a couple' and they'll tell you 'two'. But ask anybody who's had 'a couple' of drinks just how many that was and they are shamelessly unaware how bizarre the eventual clarification at 'five or six' appears to the interrogator.

A whisky is either a double, or the half-glass tumblerful one pours at home.

A bottle of cider . . . is a three-litre bottle of cider. The significance of this is paramount in such phrases as 'I had a couple of bottles of cider then went out to the pub'.

Lager is any high-alcohol-super-duper-special lager originally designed for cleaning Bavarian windows.

Wine is any fortified beverage brewed by monks vowed to secrecy and originally designed for cleaning Bavarian lager kegs.

And so on.

But the main problem with assessing alcohol intake is the scope for *self* – deception. Units of alcohol are basically simple mathematics, but the fertile mind can make it all much more compli-cated. Helped by:

a) Differences in alcoholic drinks – and an individually-accepted truth that the other guy's tipple is the dangerous one. Many patients brag 'I never drink spirits' as if this will somehow protect their liver from forty-seven pints of Guinness every night. Meantime the wine-drinker's 'couple of glasses with a meal' (particularly breakfast?) and the spirit-man's glass of whisky when he gets home (or later 'to help me sleep') will also quickly eat up the weekly allowance as a baseline before you even think of adding in the occasional pint down the pub.

b) Variation through the week. I've mentioned the 'only drink at weekends' brigade. Notwithstanding my assumption that most will drink enough during that weekend to last a giraffe for a month, I simply don't believe that people spend the rest of the week drinking no alcohol whatsoever. Why would they? Alcohol is quite nice. So the only reason to avoid it mid-week is to avoid being at work with a hangover or smelling of booze, or still drunk. Which means you don't drink bucketloads of alcohol during the week (and, by extrapolation, maybe do drink bucketloads at the week-end).

c) The times you drink the most Units are the times your brain's not best equipped to deal with big numbers . . .

This brings us to the biggest obstacle facing anybody trying to calculate their alcohol intake – all those 'helpful' Unit-values that appear in the newspapers. The 'lets-make-it-easy-for-these-stupid-people' figures that accompany articles slagging us all off for drinking in the first place. They should just tell everyone that 'One Unit' is 10 grams of alcohol (and stop changing it!) – so, for example, a litre (1000ml) of a 10% alcohol drink will have 100g of alcohol (1g = 1 ml – it's all so simple) i.e. ten Units. We could all do that sort of maths. Instead, they have all these 'one whisky = one half-pint beer = one glass of wine = one Unit' nonsense. Anybody could spot the basic flaw. As an example, one 'glass' (125ml?, 175ml?, 250ml?) of 'wine' (11%?, 12.5%?, 14.5%?) can clearly vary from 1.3 Units to 5 Units – and that's without even telling lies. The only sure thing is that it'll never be as little as one Unit. But people like to pretend it's helpful, so instead of working out they've drunk four bottles of wine in a week (quickly calculating this is about 3 litres . . . at 12% . . . 36 Units . . . oops . . .) they spend forever working out *how many glasses!* – with the clear implication that using enormous goblets from a Harry Potter movie is a sure-fire way to cut down your alcohol consumption.

It's worth mentioning here a major propaganda mistake made by the 'medical authorities' a couple of years back (that'll be at least four or five). They announced that the 'recommended upper limits' of alcohol intake per week be increased to 28 Units for men, 21 Units for women. The mistake was not that these were too high (. . . er . . . hopefully, they ain't), but that they did this at the same time their other advisors were quoting research that alcohol was quite good for you in moderate amounts . . . offering protection against stroke, heart attacks etc. I feel the general public put these two things together, somewhere in the ascending reticular formation of the collective psyche, and now view 28 Units per week not as alcohol's absolute upper limit, but as a *recommended dose.*

. . . And calories

More simple mathematics, with a bit of science. A 'calorie' is a measure of energy. When we talk about the 'calorie content' of food, we are talking about how much energy we can 'make' for ourselves by metabolising that food. We make most energy by metabolising fat, about twice as much as either carbohydrate or protein. Oddly, alcohol supplies almost as much energy as fat (the ratio fat: alcohol: carbohydrate: protein is 9:7:4:4). We then use that energy to walk, run, play football, have sex . . . and also just to *survive*, keep our hearts thumping, our bowels moving, our brains thinking (it has recently been shown that people who do puzzles and crosswords all the time lose more weight[1]). When we eat the same number of calories as we use up during the day, our weight stays the same. When we eat more, we make fat and 'lay it down' and put on weight. When we eat less, we have to delve into those stores and use them up to make the needed energy, and we lose weight. It's that simple.

As you get older and do less walking and running and playing football and having sex, you have to learn to eat less if you want to stay the same weight. Or deliberately do some replacement exercise (though if you can't walk, can't run . . .). And the

[1] Other things being equal. Not suggesting they're skinnier than marathon-runners.

big, important word there is 'OR'. Not 'AND'. You can keep things under control by either eating less OR doing more exercise. You don't need both. The second-biggest propaganda mistake medics (who are these people?) ever made was to tell the punters (that's you) that exercise is good for you and helps you lose weight. This was immediately interpreted that you could *only* lose weight if you did more exercise. So, since then, all my fat patients blame their fatness on not being able to exercise. 'I can't lose weight, my knee's too sore.' Or (genuine) 'I put on a stone over Christmas because the weather was so bad'.

Time for a tip.

Top Tip No 5
Not exercising does not make you fat.

It's the food that does it – or, at least, the imbalance. You cannot bring down your exercise quotient so much that you will gain weight despite eating 'next-to-nothing, Doctor'. It takes hundreds of calories just to keep your body alive during the day. Or, as I tell patients to their great confusion or disgust, *the problems of a famine in Africa will NOT be solved by telling them to play less football.*

So next time your doctor suggests that since you weigh eighteen stones and your knees are killing you, perhaps you might like to try lose some weight, don't tell him you 'eat hardly anything'. He won't believe you. He doesn't believe all the others. Maybe you eat less than you used to, maybe no more than a normal-sized person, but if you are continuing to gain weight then at this point in time you are eating more than you are using up and are therefore *eating too much*.[2]

One last analogy to explain this. Let's go back to the garage, this time for petrol. Every week you put twenty litres into your car's tank. But this week the twentieth litre overflows all over your new jeans (OK – the cut-off gizmo isn't working, for dramatic effect) because the tank's full. The attendant suggests maybe you're not using the car as much (no longer driving to the gym . . .), so you should put less petrol in. What do you do? Do you argue that 20 litres isn't too much petrol for a week so it must be OK? Do you argue you're not actually putting in 20 litres . . . indeed you're hardly putting any petrol in at all and it must be overflowing because your car has suddenly developed some special engine which travels for miles and miles and uses up hardly any petrol . . .? Or do you just *put less petrol in?*

---

[2] Caveat. An underactive thyroid slows down metabolism and you can gain weight despite eating less. But a) doctors always check for it as soon as weight gain raises its ugly head, so b) we should never have mentioned it since now some patients insist they must have a special undiagnosable form of hypothyroidism though c) even with slow metabolism you'll still lose weight if you reduce your food intake enough. Even Hypothyroid Man cannot *create* energy.

So if your doctor doesn't seem to believe that you eat 'hardly anything', don't hold it against him. As a quasi-scientist, he's wedded to the mathematics of the situation. Look instead at why he doesn't think your appraisal is accurate, and it doesn't really matter whether you eventually tell him how much you really eat or not, as long as you tell yourself.

KNOW YOUR ENEMY

Hospital Doctors

If you want to keep your hospital consultant happy, it's important to know a bit about the world they live in.

Physicians vs Surgeons

Hospital doctors divide uneasily into two categories. Physicians and surgeons.

OK, there are some others. Anaesthetists, for example – but we can forget about trying to keep them happy for three good reasons:

a) Any personal contact with anaesthetists should be kept to a minimum (mainly because anaesthesia is dangerous – though the advice does hold at the social level).

b) Anaesthetists don't actually have emotions, so wouldn't understand what happiness was. They do, after all, abandon the traditional touchy-feely world of doctoring to spend a maximum of ten seconds with any patient, using that time to teach them how to count backwards from ten.

c) When there *is* contact, 'keeping them happy' consists of shutting up and going to sleep very quickly

So don't argue. Let's keep it simple and start again.

Physicians *and* surgeons

Physicians are the medical doctors. They look after heart attacks[1] (which they call 'myocardial infarctions' just to remind you who's boss) and strokes and pneumonias and chronic bronchitises and blood-poisoning ('septicaemia') and liver disease and arthritis and overdoses and all that sort of stuff.

Surgeons cut things out. It's parental conditioning really – that's what they were always told as a child.

The two groups may be trickier to distinguish, however, if they are not performing these tasks when you meet them (e.g. at a cocktail party,

[1] Political correctness mandates I should say 'patients *with* heart-attacks', but this is inaccurate. Nurses, physios, porters etc look after patients and doctors really do only look after the diseases.

though here less problematic since any surgeon not being paid enough attention will immediately remind people exactly who he is . . .), so knowledge of other features will be required.

The scenario in which you encounter them may be an aid in itself. Surgeons may be busy playing golf, or baring one nipple while kneeling with head bowed – but then, so might the more ambitious physician. Physical attributes and abilities may also help. Physicians are the ones who are tall and thin, can pronounce words properly, enunciate fully formed sentences, count up to ten without using their fingers (and toes) . . . and tie their own shoelaces. Surgeons aren't.[2]

It is of course dangerous to pigeon-hole someone entirely based on demographics. Rheumatoid arthritis is much more common in women, but only a really stupid doctor would allow that to stop him from diagnosing it in a man. Footballers are thought to be thuggish and not-particularly-bright, but that doesn't make Thierry Henry a cricketer. However, these warnings aside, I still think it worthwhile to outline the main features that help distinguish physicians and surgeons in Table 1.

[2] Except that surgeons can, of course, tie their own shoe-laces – very well indeed – though they need a pair of small sharp scissors to untie them.

TABLE 1

Physicians (Male)	Surgeons (Male)
Tall and thin	Short and squat
Wear unpolished loafers/thick-soled Clark's shoes	Big black shiny shoes with thin leather soles that go clippety-clop on the ward floor
Wear loosely-fitting tie[3]	Wear pin-striped tie with knot fastened by a butler[3]
Wanted to bowl for Hampshire	Wanted to hook for Wasps[4]

Physicans (Female)	Surgeons (Female)
Tall and thin	Short and squat
Don't wear ties at all	Occasionally wear tie around head
Wear ethnic earrings with lots of dangly gold and garnets	Wear tiny stud earrings that won't flop into patient's innards. No garnets (if do fall off, you'll never find them)
Place is full of them	Her name is Helen

[3] Since writing, ties have been banned as an infection-risk in many hospitals . . . as have butlers.
[4] Like fly-fishing for trout but trickier.

Physicians (Both)	Surgeons (Both)
Wear glasses for reading (kept in pocket)	Wear glasses for making them look intellectual (kept on odd elastic metal-thingy round neck)
Never actually make a diagnosis	Know what's wrong with patient the minute it (sic) points to somewhere on its (sick) body
Never can decide what to do next	Knows immediately what to do next (but can't remember what they did last)
Order lots of investigations in case they're missing something	Order lots of physicians in case they're missing something[5]
Never actually make anything better	Half the time make things better. Half the time make things worse.

This pigeon-holing looms HUGE in the minds of both physicians and surgeons. And since doctors are more prone than most to the

[5] Initially had 'order lots of pizza and beer' but didn't want to appear flippant.

world-revolves-around-me mind-set, they assume that every lay person knows about it. So when you ask a hospital doctor at a dinner party (after making mental note to vet your invites more carefully) what's his specialty and he says 'medicine' don't assume he's being cheeky. He is happily informing you that he is smart, thoughtful, considerate – and not a thug (the more perspicacious among you will have spotted to which camp the author belongs – that's why he uses words like 'perspicacious'). Of course, he may be a surgeon trying to pretend that he's smart, thoughtful and considerate, but this is unlikely since a) the general population doesn't realise this significance, rendering the deception pointless, and b) neither do surgeons. But they do know they're in a different league (though they confuse which one's the Premiership). And they expect you to know this. And we both expect you to realise that physicians resent surgeons and vice-versa.

Physicians resent surgeons because they know physicians are the smart ones, but the surgeons get all the kudos from the public and the Press. (Why? Well, what's more exciting; slicing a dying man's chest open and ripping out a chunk of blood-stained goo, or listening to his heart, wrinkling an eyebrow and giving him a pink tablet?)

Surgeons resent physicians for . . . exactly the same reason. Like the guy who steals an invention – or the idea for a play – resents the person they stole it from; because the other guy *knows* . . .

★　★　★

We should take time-out here to consider one side-issue of the above which requires explanation.

The 'Mister' mystery.

Surgeons have fancy exams they have to pass on the way to consultanthood. Organised by the Royal Colleges, they are taken after 3–6 years of being a qualified doctor. Successful candidates drop the 'Doctor' and revert to 'Mister'. Physicians, on the other hand, pass their fancy exams and stick with 'Doctor'. The exams are equally fancy, but the fact that surgeons change to Mister has been picked up on by the general public as the hallmark of a major career advance. A new level of expertise. Since the physician doesn't change his title, promotion does not carry the recognition in the general population to which he feels entitled. This makes physicians very bitter. They will therefore delight in explaining to anyone who'll listen that the reason for the 'Mister' harks back to the days when surgeons weren't doctors at all – but barbers. Medically-trained people did all that clever thinking and examining stuff to see what was wrong with you, but you went to a barber if you needed anything hacked out.[6] So the surgeons were 'Misters' and this title has been retained, essentially as an affectation. It does result in some problems – e.g. as to what female surgeons should

[6] First choice was obviously butchers, but they couldn't stop chopping every organ they came across into neat slices and sticking a pointy-sign through it.

call themselves Having your coronary artery bypass performed by a Mrs McGinty just doesn't sound right.

So.

Don't call your physician 'Mister' (if you do and are somehow informed of your mistake, don't slag him off for being 'still just a doctor at your age . . .' whether seeing him professionally or socially[7]). And don't call your surgeon 'Doctor', unless he looks like he's twelve. Getting the terminology right can prevent any . . . unpleasantness. Not confusing their actual jobs also helps. As a rheumatologist, I am occasionally flummoxed by a patient who not only calls me 'Mister' but also expects me to replace their gammy hip with a new one. I try to explain that rheumatologists don't put in new hips, but modify the pain in the old ones (just like a physiotherapist, only we make it *less*), but they still insist on showing me pictures from an internet catalogue and asking whether titanium or vanadium would be best.

Even in the workplace, identifying the two opposing camps isn't always easy. Particularly if they do not fulfil the stereotypes in incredibly helpful, but

[7] Happened to me at the bridge club. ('No, he's not a Mister, he's still a doctor. He hasn't reached those high echelons yet.') Though what anyone thought a surgeon might be doing at a bridge club escapes me . . . maybe fixing a table leg.

ultimately flawed Table 1. Surgeons do not walk around the place with a sign on their forehead saying 'I am a surgeon' (though many would like to). So you have to learn to spot them. It can boil down to whereabouts they are in the hospital. Clearly a guy in the surgical clinic will tend to be a surgeon and so on (later we'll see how this doesn't pertain for surgical wards). But even if you can literally read the signs, you'll have to know what specialties are surgical.

Surgeons include the guys working in general surgery, cardiothoracic surgery, bowel surgery, breast surgery, neurosurgery – you'll have noted a recurring clue, but orthopaedics and Ear Nose and Throat (ENT) are surgical too. Medical specialties include cardiology, respiratory medicine, gastro-enterology, neurology, rheumatology, endocrinology, haematology and dermatology. Basically anything with '-ology', except gynaecology and ophthalmology which lie somewhere between medicine and surgery. Most *doctors* can never remember whether to call them 'Mister' or 'Doctor'. So while your gastroenterologist may diagnose ulcerative colitis and ask a colonic surgeon to do any required operation if drug therapy fails, the eye doctor who prescribes drugs will be the same one who actually attacks your peepers with micro-mini-scalpels when the tablets let him down.

I'll mention anaesthetists again, as they are even more difficult to classify. They are known as

'Doctor' – that's easy. They're just . . . difficult to classify.

Once you've used the above handy hints to spot who is who (we'll deal with GPs later), the next step in keeping all of them happy is learning some of their individual traits.

SURGICAL SPECIALTIES

General Surgery

The first thing to remember about general surgeons is that they're not very bright. We spot them early at Med School. They're the big bruisers who jump in first when it comes to chopping up frogs, rats . . . or indeed people, but who are posted missing when it comes to spelling aspirin. They smoked like chimneys, drank like anti-freeze was going out of fashion (which, fortunately, it was), and would impress girls at parties by eating glass tumblers or lighting their farts, or both.[1] They played rugby for the third fifteen (since the firsts weren't allowed to drink beer during a match, and the seconds only at half-time), went to the gym for weight-training in place of lectures, and only went to the library if the gym was shut and they had to make do with pushing bookshelves through the wall.

Unfortunately, for some reason, their non-brightness isn't so evident in later years – particularly

[1] Originally I wrote this as 'tried to impress' . . . but unfortunately it worked.

to the lay public who generally believe surgeons to be top dogs in the profession. But remember it. Do not attempt to chummy up with some patter on Marcel Proust, or Gustav Flaubert and the merits of early realism in nineteenth century France. Unless Gustav plans to sign for Arsenal, our surgical hero will not have the slightest clue what you're on about. Football, rugby, golf, and a smattering of information on the stockmarket (viz-a-viz how it affects HIM) is about the limit.

The second thing to remember is that the first thing relates to *all* surgeons. Some odd beliefs have sprouted in the general populace that, for example, *brain* surgeons are clever. There is no logic to this. Is a garage mechanic working on a Mercedes more handsome than one working on a Ford? (or a French teacher a better cook than an English teacher?) Makes no sense. Yet there is a tendency to associate the doctor with the bit of the body that he works on, or knows about. Thus rheumatologists are slow and cumbersome, geriatricians are old and decrepit, and . . . brain surgeons are clever.[2]

The chattering classes seem happy to perpetuate the myth. If you read Ian McEwan's *Saturday* (not that I'd for a moment suggest you should) you'll discover the brain-surgeon protagonist knows every little detail about the brain's function, down to the transmission of single molecules between

[2] This might also explain one opinion of gastro-enterologists – though not why it's held by doctors.

individual cells. He walks the streets of London, obsessing over how this simple action is effected by his axon endings releasing glutamic acid residues which cross the synapse to bind receptors on the membrane of the . . . etc. Every doctor who reads this giggles out loud. Every neurosurgeon they know is more likely to walk the streets reciting the mnemonic his mum taught him when he was little . . . 'LTRTLTRTLTRT' . . . to remind him which order to use his feet in.[3]

Orthopaedic Surgery

Orthopaedic surgeons make general surgeons look like Mastermind candidates. At Uni, they played (as a forward, of course) for the first rugby XV since everybody was too scared to stop them drinking beer during the game. No-one ever knew their real name as they changed it every week to avoid being banned *sine die* – a constant worry since they treated rugby matches as practice for their weekends with the Territorial Army.[4]

---

[3] Since you ask, it stands for 'Then' – otherwise he'll try using both left and right at the same time.

[4] Or vice-versa. One colleague would proudly describe a 'sport' from TA training where the rules were simple – there were NO rules. Absolutely none. Do-what-you-like. He was particularly proud since the only time he played the game he was disqualified.

Once qualified it becomes clear that their chosen specialty is better served by a big pair of strong hands than a big pair of cerebral cortices. Most will therefore work on further downgrading their intellectual abilities, reducing any contact with the outside world (patients) to single-word sentences as they prod you about with minimal preliminaries (get them to say *that* out loud):

'*Hi.*'

'*Hi.*'

'*Fell?*'

'*Yes.*'

'*Sore?*'

'*Yes.*'

'*Here?*'

'*Yiaaaaaigh!*'

'*Or here?*'

'*Nnnnghyiaghiiii!*'

'*Or both?*'

'*Yiaaaaaigh! Nnnnghyiaghiiii!*'

'*Theatre 6, Nurse!*'

The only drawback to this minimalist approach occurs in the private sector (Q: How do you hide a tenner from an orthopaedic surgeon? A: Hold it in the hand that isn't sore).

Don't try to talk to them about anything other than sport.

Top Tip No 6
Don't shake hands.

Obstetricians & Gynaecologists

This is a challenge. Smart-alec observations without stepping over the line for what is decent and acceptable. It's obvious that obstetricians and gynaecologists (usually the same guys, and, oddly enough, usually guys) must be tremendously focused individuals. As a medical student finishing my first week in gynaecology I was struck by the fact that a hitherto sacrosanct part of the female anatomy with which I had less than minimum previous acquaintance had, in five short days, by myself been . . .

   a) stared at
   b) rummaged about in
   c) observed via a short-range telescope (colposcopy)
   d) scraped gently with a blunt skelf of wood
   e) scraped vigorously with a tiny but very sharp spoon

. . . before Friday afternoon's finale which I spent inserting radioactive rods . . . (a bizarre anti-cancer therapy). Indeed one beleaguered colleague commented after a taxing cervical smear clinic that he'd 'seen more fannies than you could shake a stick at.' (where's that line I was talking about? . . .)

Clearly gynaecologists, even more than other doctors, must be able to blot out from their minds what it is they are actually doing. This talent unfortunately interferes with their conversational abilities, and they have a tendency to stare at the horizon and not quite catch what you are saying. Any attempts at pleasantries or asides concerning the real world are likely to go straight over their heads, since, as a patient, that's the way you'd want to keep it. In the social scenario, however, they're handy people to know only if you've lost your keys in your handbag.

Accident & Emergency Specialists

Even in a book designed to keep your doctor happy, I find myself making space for self-preservation advice entirely for *your* benefit (can't shake off that whole 'Hippocratic Oath' thing). Your attendance at the Casualty Department (or A&E) is such a potentially devastating event that keeping the doctor happy struggles to remain our main priority. I feel obliged to let you into an important secret.

Top Tip No 7
The doctor who sees you in Casualty is NOT wondering what's wrong with you. He's wondering who he's going to get to look after you.

It's his *raison d'etre*. They've got all these four-hour-rules and things – not that they care how long a patient has to wait, more that they need to make space for the next one. It's basically the same as being the tidying-up person at McDonald's. So, to clear his department of all unwanted detritus (patients), he has to direct you onto the care of a physician, general surgeon, orthopaedic surgeon or whatever. And while it doesn't matter one iota to him whether you are *triaged* onto the right person or a passing window-cleaner, to you it may be crucial. Most of the time the decision is obvious (e.g pneumonias to physicians, appendices to surgeons, footballers to orthopaedics[5]), but a number of presentations can be ambiguous – particularly at the boundaries of medicine and surgery. And since surgeons are big butch guys with loud voices and physicians are big girls' blouses with girls' blouses, and neither wants to do more work than they have to, Casualty doctors find it easier to channel borderline patients towards the medical team. Indeed it's worth their while to 'massage' the symptoms of clearly surgical cases to foist them upon the physicians (usually something that doesn't require an immediate operation – they're not actually evil). So as a consultant physician, I find myself looking after patients with gall-stones whose upper-tummy pains the A&E man describes as 'lower-chest pain – maybe a heart

---

[5] Even if they've had a heart-attack. Send them to coronary care and their agent will complain they're not getting enough scans.

attack'. Make the abdominal pain further down, and give it some vomiting and they're in trouble – that's *clearly* surgical . . . but help is at hand. By some traditional quirk most hospitals get physicians to look after (at least initially) a bleed from a duodenal or stomach ulcer. If the A&E man can persuade a patient to concede they *might* have had blood in their vomit ('haematemesis'), then they can pretend it's medical and shuffle the patient off to the medical wards. It's easier than spending all afternoon trying to page the on-call surgeon out of theatre (they're *always* in theatre, even when there hasn't been a patient brought in during the last fortnight to operate on). Since blood-in-the-vomit can look browny-black (classically 'like coffee-grounds') when it's been lying in the stomach for a while (an effect of the acid), they can usually get a patient to admit to something of the sort.

My favourite (genuine!) recent example was a man hit on the back of his head with a baseball bat. He developed a major headache (duh!) and vomiting. A&E held onto him while the vomiting continued . . . eventually becoming that dirty bilestained stuff we all get if we keep vomiting. 'Coffee-grounds!!!' the A&E staff cried in triumph and presented him to my juniors[6] as a 'haematemesis'.

---

[6] OK . . . nowadays we're all a *team* . . . shouldn't call them my juniors . . . but have you seen the age of them?

So what's the point of telling you all this? Well, for one, it gets the rant off my chest. For two, it lets you know about triage – a term which was originally used in France for the pigeon-holing of wounded soldiers into those who had a chance of surviving and those who didn't, thus giving priority to those who had *less* severe injuries (unless really trivial – that's back in the 'can wait' category). But for three, it is also possible that you can use this info to make sure you yourself get sent to the right place. How do you know where that is? Not that difficult. In the good old days, it wasn't the A&E doctors who decided where a patient-off-the-street would go. It was the porters. As junior first-on-call physician I'd be wakened at three in the morning by a phone call from Billy at the front desk. 'Chest pain, Doc,' was all he needed to say and up I'd jump. Same thing with breathlessness, headache (not caused by baseball bat), seizures, weakness (stroke) or swelling in the legs (deep vein thrombosis, cellulitis) which were all obviously medical. When I became a surgical resident[7], I would be wakened by 'pain in the abdomen' or (my favourite) 'condition of lower body, Doc'. Basically there was a 'surgical window' of problems between your diaphragm and just below your groin, and

[7] First year as a doctor, we all did six months of each. Medicine and surgery. Like joining the Dallas Cowboys, doing one term as quarter-back and one as a line-backer before deciding what suits.

everything else was medical unless it was caused by trauma (as in getting-hit-by-bus trauma, not boy-friend-has-chucked-me trauma).

And it worked. The porters were almost always right. You can do the same thing. If the casualty doctor says he's sending you to the medical ward because he thinks the excruciating pain and tenderness over your appendix is caused by pneumonia – ask to see a surgeon. If he says the reason you can't walk is because the motor-bike that hit you has set off your diabetes – ask to see a surgeon. If he asks if there was anything that looked like coffee-grounds in your vomit, remind him that *everybody* who keeps vomiting gets 'coffee-grounds', so why does he want to know?

But if he does get the surgeons to look after you . . . ask to see a physician as well, just in case. They are, after all, the doctors (and you might need more than a shave).

Oh yeah. And if, for some reason, you want to keep your A&E doctor happy, just forget everything I said.

ENT Surgeons

The only people who don't go around trying to remember if Grommet's the dog. The way to keep them happy is never, ever, to admit that you put cotton buds in your ear (they push the wax back and concertina it and maybe damage the eardrum and maybe induce infection . . .) – even though that's the only reason any of us ever buys them.

Neurosurgeons

To keep them happy, just make like you're unconscious. They like it that way. Makes them the smartest guy in the room.

Or you could ask them to describe what brain cells do when you're walking . . .

MEDICAL SPECIALTIES

Cardiologists

Cardiologists deal with the heart. The nearest medical equivalents to the surgical up-and-at-'em psyche, they take a brief history, wave a stethoscope vaguely in your direction (if they've remembered to bring one – the modern cardiologist only actually listens through a stethoscope if he's lost the combination to his safe) before organising a couple of scans and exercise tests and stuff that tell them the answers. Since these tests are all performed by the cardiologist himself, they do tremendously well in the private sector (hence the safe). Particularly since everyone, including the insurance companies, worries overmuch about the heart (whereas I agree with Woody Allen that it should be, at best, your third most favourite organ) and will happily cough up oodles of cash to pay a bill of clean health.

Cardiologists are thus pretty well-heeled, and fairly cocky about their position in the medical pecking-order. But they like it confirmed, so flattery will get you most places. On the whole, however, they are none too bright[1], so don't keep it subtle. Try not to make too many references to cultural pursuits like art or literature, as they're unlikely to follow. Think of them as a surgeon who's read a book once.

Cardiologists, I should also explain, insist that any paragraph containing the word 'cardiologist' must have this as first word; no other word should ever precede it. Just in case you thought I was being a bit slack with my literary technique.

Respiratory Physicians

Respiratory physicians look after your lungs. It's OK to call them 'chest doctors' – cardiologists don't get upset. They tend to cut a more desolate figure than the buoyant cardiologist, having universally failed to get over the psychological scarring of two major drawbacks in their chosen profession.

One is that while the lungs are clearly every bit as important as the heart (what's the point of pumping all that blood around your body if there's no oxygen in it?) nobody seems to care. Chest physicians are seen as the poor cousins of cardiologists, despite the lungs (with all their fiddly transport mechanisms of oxygen and

---

[1] An unfounded and uncalled-for dig made out of sheer jealousy on my part – for which I apologise profusely and which I retract unreservedly. (I assume by this time you've given up reading the footnotes).

carbon dioxide across membranes and things) being much trickier and more complex than the heart, which is basically a pump that any competent central heating engineer could fix in his sleep. They did have a brief period in vogue back in the day, when TB ravaged the world and their talents were desperately sought to save such luminaries as Frederic Chopin, Mimi and The lady of The Camellias. But you'll have spotted these examples all share one feature (hmm . . . and it's not that they're all real people . . .) in that after the respiratory guys were called in to cure them . . . they all *died* of the disease. It's all very well being the trendy specialist to look after a trendy malady, but when you can do naff-all to help, and all your patients die, your fame soon palls. By the time they had some decent drugs to combat TB, the BCG vaccine and sanitary improvements were pretty much eradicating the disease – at least from the rich and important, who were unfortunately the rich and important ones.

The second drawback is that most info on the lungs is gained by examining from the back – so no excuse for a free peek at Mimi's heavingly ample bosoms.

There is, however, a silver lining. Despite the major sadness and complexity of these individuals' psyche, it is relatively easy to keep them relatively happy.

Just don't smoke.

Leabharlanna Poibli Chathair Bhaile Átha Cliath
Dublin City Public Libraries

Gastroenterologists

Spend their lives sticking tubes up and down things that were never designed to have tubes stuck up and down them. Endoscopies to see if the patient has a peptic ulcer, and 'sigmoidoscopies' to see if they have colitis. And both to see if they have anything nasty. Their favourite phrase for describing a patient who requires both is that they need 'top-and-tailed'. Their favourite phrase when speaking to such patients is 'just relax', invariably at times when that isn't humanly possible.

The best way to keep them happy is to eat absolutely nothing for the three days before you are due for either topping or tailing, or both. Think of Harry Lime running through the sewers of Vienna . . . if they were *full*.

Rheumatologists

Look after your joints. Ostensibly. Unless you've got a 'proper' arthritis like rheumatoid, they're really not interested. So if you've got wear-and-tear osteoarthritis – even if you're screaming all night with the pain – I wouldn't bother. You'd be as well letting your GP look after it. He can tell you to lose weight, swim, do muscle-building exercises, Yoga, Tai Chi . . . as well as the next man. And since the next man will be an orthopaedic surgeon, I'd listen to what he's saying. Not that the orthopaedic surgeon is useless in this scenario. He'll do what he always does . . . replace the joint nearest the pain. And if by happy coincidence that's what's causing it, you'll be fine.

If you want to keep your rheumatologist happy, you should arrange to have one of the 'interesting' rheumatic diseases such as a Connective Tissue Disease or one of the 'vasculitides'. These make up less than 1% of their patient load, but 90% of their research efforts and 95% of their coffee-room chat (the other 5% is to complain about the coffee).

Endocrinologists

Diabetes, thyroid disease and other hormone stuff. The diagnosis and management of these problems depends almost entirely on monitoring blood results, so you can keep them happy just by having big veins, and being impressed by anyone with even an elementary grasp of mathematics.

Oh, and tell the truth about whether you're taking the tablets. This is important with all specialties, but in endocrinology – where it's all down to the numbers – even more so, since they won't try something different. They'll just keep upping and upping your dosage until you're 'taking' a kilogram of thyroid hormone per day and when you come into hospital for your hernia operation they'll 'carry on' at 'the same' dosage; but now you'll really be getting it . . .

Neurologists

Brain and nerves and things like that. Traditionally, they like to precisely diagnose small-print neurological disorders which you can't treat. This suits them as they can't be bothered with all that making-you-better nonsense. They have been known to panic at the threatened introduction of a new drug designed to treat a disease which is well-established as untreatable. Keep them happy by turning up punctiliously for your first clinic consultation and MRI brain scan, then failing to attend any further appointments.[2]

Top Tip No 8
Keep in with anybody in any of the above groups by slagging off anybody in any other groups. If spoilt for choice, pick surgeons or cardiologists. That'll please most people.

---

[2] Hmmm . . . keeps them happy, but maybe not you. Might even be a potentially dangerous plan.

STUDENTS

The first thing to remember about medical students is that you are not obliged to see them. When the doctor asks if you are happy for his rag-bag of variously-pierced monsters to come in and examine you (as he should – but sometimes forgets), you are entirely at liberty to come out with a polite 'no, thanks'. No-one will take offence – though it's probably worth not turning your nose up too obviously. Indeed the refusal might well be keeping the doctor happy. If it's an official bedside-teaching session, then the doctor wants you to say yes, otherwise he has to find another victim. But if it's a student tagging along as he's doing his clinic/ward-round, that won't be the case. As a jobbing whateverologist, you quickly realise that they are quite a hassle:

a) You're expected to teach them (when you're *busy*, seeing patients and stuff).
b) They ask awkward questions. At formal teaching, it's easy for a doctor to ask students questions to which they won't know the answer, but when 'shadowing',

it's almost as easy for students to do the same thing – and that direction is much less fun, and tricky to sidestep in front of a patient.

c) Their very presence means that as a consultant you have to alter your examination technique. All my short-cuts go out the window. Listening to chests through the patient's shirt . . . prodding tummies while they're sitting in a chair[1] . . . assessing knees through a pair of baggy jeans . . . all scuppered. As is sneaking down to the canteen while the juniors get on with the clinic in the naïf belief that you're struggling behind the closed doors of your consulting-room with a particularly tricky diagnostic dilemma.

So just say no, and the doctor will probably be over the moon. So will the student. Instead of being a rabbit in the headlights of the chief's quick-fire questions, they can run off to aforementioned canteen, where they and the consultant can stare into their respective coffees, studiously failing

---

[1] The abdomen should be examined with the patient lying relaxed, flat on their back. An old surgical adage added 'with the abdomen bared from the nipples to the knees' but that's the usual triumph of adroit alliteration over common sense. And indeed the usual triumph of surgeons over common sense. Or common decency.

to notice the other's presence. You, the patient, also get *your* way – so everybody's happy. Except, of course, some years down the line, all the newly-qualified doctors will be carrying out critical diagnostic examinations, never having before seen a patient with their jacket off.

So what we're looking for is some sort of balance. You don't want to be abused, but neither do you want to stand in the way of genuine medical education.

And there is something to consider.

Why, exactly, do none of us (including me) want to be examined by students? It's not likely that they will physically damage you (though the occasional ham-fisted 'percussion' of the chest wall does look like it could crack one of Mike Tyson's ribs), nor that their prognostications will affect your treatment – though stranger things have happened. An A&E colleague once roped-in the help of the ubiquitous callow youth to stitch up a simple head wound, whilst she went off to attend a stand-by:

Student, yeah?
Yeah.
What year you in?
Fourth.
Should be able to cope with this, then. Stitch that up for me and I'll be back in ten minutes

I hope you've spotted the mistake. It was the terminology that undid her. Like me, she thought of schoolkids as *'pupils'*, so when the youngster said he was a fourth year student, it didn't occur to her that this meant he was a fifteen-year-old on work experience.

But actual suffering at the hands of a student is unlikely – the petrified but focussed teenager probably did a better stitching job than a hurried casualty officer. And basically it comes down to this. We don't want to expose stuff to an 'unqualified practitioner'. The reason is unclear. There's no magical transformation when someone picks up their medical degree, no angel dust which simultaneously makes them immune to the horrors of a skeleton-infested cupboard, or the attractions of perfectly-formed pert breasts . . .

But that's what it's about. Breasts, groins and secrets.

Breasts

We'll take breasts first. My theory is that, no matter how hard they try to avoid it, women will always have a fear that this guy is getting some sort of kick out of seeing their naked body (and that bit about pert breasts probably didn't help . . .). Arguably, the usual awkward embarrassment of students seeing unclothed patients might suggest the exact opposite. More nervous rabbits in headlights. They're too busy trying to think of what they're supposed to do, and in what order, and *just any* diagnosis that could possibly fit, to think of anything else. However, the suspicion does seem to be there. And a number of idiosyncrasies of students' examination technique only add to the worries. It might therefore be of some help in allaying such fears for me to explain that:

1) medical students are taught to 'observe first, then examine.' For instance, in examining the chest, look for breath-lessness, deformity in the chest wall, asymmetry in the breathing etc. before percussing or getting out your stetho-scope. This is why the young Goth with the nose-ring will help you get your top and bra off, sit you up against the nicely-organised pillows, then walk down to the foot of the bed and for all the world clearly stare at your boobs.

2) When examining the heart, they will put their hands flat against the area of the chest/breast overlying each of the heart valves. A simple test. A damaged heart valve will buzz – a bit like a cat's purr – and this has a possibly unfortunate technical term. When he therefore tells the doctor-superior-examiner person that he is 'feeling for thrills', this should not disconcert you. Though any inclusion of superfluous adjectives such as 'cheap' might raise some suspicions.

Groins

Here boy-patients also require handling with kid-gloves (preferably latex-coated). Again, it's worth knowing that all students are taught that examination of the abdomen includes examining the groin for lymph nodes ('glands' qv) and for the pulse of the femoral artery in the groin. The awkwardness of this with either sex whilst trying NOT TO TOUCH ANYTHING explains why half-the-time we fail to find the femoral pulse despite the artery being ten times the size of the one at the wrist. More 'intimate'[2] examination of females in this area is not carried out by students without your expressed consent, and these days only if the student is actively involved in your management. I say 'these days' as in the past, the general axiom elsewhere in the body that students should 'feel as many normal ones as you can so you get used to it' was thought to hold true even of the more intimate areas.

For women, intimate examination will almost always occur when attending a gynaecologist, so you will to some extent be 'prepared', but occasionally the male's nether regions will feature as part of the examination by a general physician. Whether this is simply part of the modern culture of who-cares-what-a-man-thinks – which we guys

---

[2] Standard euphemism for vaginal examination – blithely ignoring the total lack of intimacy that is a pre-requisite.

are obliged to accept as 'progress' – or a genuine reflection of males being more blasé about such things, is unclear. Either way the necessity for such examinations almost always takes a chap by surprise – rather like Chandler's visit to Joey's tailor in *Friends* ('Yes Joey, that *is* the way they measure you for pants . . . in prison!'). Yet pointers elsewhere in the history or examination might make it a requirement. Most practitioners find this every bit as embarrassing as the patient does, so we offer both patient and ourselves a way out by asking 'do you examine yourself (i.e. your testicles) regularly?' to which you reply 'oh yes, of course' and everybody's happy. Unless, of course, you don't really, and there was something really important to discover and we've missed it through embarrassment.

Similarly, in the (good) old days, any self-respecting woman seeing any self-respecting doctor about a problem above the ankles would have her breasts examined 'while we're at it' (not the recommended phraseology). But nowadays there's increasing awareness of how 'invasive' this is, and many doctors replace it with a 'do you examine your breasts every month?' and you can keep him happy and relieved by saying yes. And the big question is, do early lumps get missed? Indeed I've often wondered if the entire don't-look-at-her-breasts-more-than-you-have-to thing leads to women's chests, hearts and lungs all being universally less-well examined than men's because doctors want to avoid causing embarrassment. I wouldn't dream of examining a man's heart through his vest (unless I'm in a hurry), but we all think twice before getting a woman to remove her bra. Another upshot is that I preferentially go to male patients if I am teaching 'on the chest'. So students get even less chance to learn how to deal with the problem, and women – just maybe – get under-examined for evermore.

Secrets

We don't really want to tell anybody if we drink too much alcohol, smoke too many cigarettes, snort too much cocaine, run around with too many ladies-of-the-night – but it might crop up when you're talking to your doctor. I can understand extra reluctance if it's a student-doctor, but it's ill-placed. The whole confidentiality-thing holds true every bit as much for them, and if they did break the rules, it'd be easier to haul them over the coals than an Oxbridge professor. It would be unusual for the overseeing doctor to put you in this situation, so it may be he was simply unaware of any problem. Which brings us right back to the beginning.

It's OK to just say no.

The above gives you just a glimpse into the workings of the student mind. I hope it brings some reassurance. They're usually more unsettled than you are. Later we will go into their examination technique in more detail, this time more proactively, in the chapter on 'Getting Your Own Back'.

GIFTS

The problem of gifts for your doctor is not especially tricky. It's not like:

a) Taxi-drivers
b) Waiters
c) Hairdressers

in

A) France
B) Portugal
C) Czech Republic

where you have to remember whether to tip not-at-all (aB), tip only slightly by rounding-up (bA, bB, aC, bC), tip hugely (aA, cA) – or avoid using their services all together since you're never too far away from a World Cup (cB) or a wedding (cC). Any incorrect algebra would of course be dangerously insulting.

No.

The simple, safe fall-back position is that you never need give your doctor any present of any sort. That will always be the norm. Doctors do, of course, get gifts from one source – drug reps. New rules are being constantly introduced to limit these, since clearly any doctor would start prescribing Limecycline if you bribed him with a cuckoo clock. Trinkets, therefore, should be worth less than a fiver (pens not to be supplied by Mont Blanc). Hospitality – meals or hotel accommodation for conferences – should never be 'at a level of expense the doctors wouldn't normally pay for themselves' – which is why once a year I make a point of taking the missus somewhere decent. But the only *patients* who tend to give doctors gifts are other doctors when they find themselves on the wrong side of the fence.

Indeed you could argue there is no place at all for this chapter. I shouldn't confuse people by suggesting for a moment that a gift for the doctor is in any way normal or expected. However, my title for this treatise is 'How to keep Your Doctor Happy' and bearing gifts has historically fulfilled that function. Bright shiny beads and firewater (worth less than five Apache dollars). Regarding medics, it goes along with the rose-tinted vision of a rural GP, stalwart of the community, friend and confidante as well as consummate professional. We've all seen it on TV. The local rustics are forever bringing him an apple pie, a wrigglingly fresh salmon, or even fresher leg of lamb ('Fluffy would have wanted you to have this . . .'). Back in the big bad city, a gentle gift that somehow relates to the patient's occupation or interests can have the same congenial effect. A box of sweets from a shop-keeper, buns from a baker, coke from the local supplier (sorry . . . 'Coke'). To some extent it's a financial thing. Doctors earn more than most people, so the most 'acceptable' sort of present is one that costs the donor less than the object's actual value. Less awkward, and more efficient.

For the rest of us, where such a gift is unavailable, it is a bit more tricky. There's no point in me gift-wrapping a plastizote wrist-splint (except for the unsuspecting kids at Christmas – 'Look Peter! It can be an aeroplane!'). Home baking is, of course, ever welcome – though I am always careful to check exactly how well I dealt with that partic-ular patient's case . . . usually I let the nurses have some first. Home knitting, craft-work and paintings pose different problems, as you don't wish to appear ungrateful. Doctors' coffee-rooms are notoriously full of knitted gnomes, matchstick cottages or mixed-media-seas-capes-made-entirely-from-the-flotsam-on-Turnberry-Sands, but we sometimes get our own back and display them in the waiting-room. It is acceptable for such self-made offerings to be elaborate, with creative references to the world of medicine or even the patient's illness. Indeed the more elaborate, the better. The more elaborate they are, the more unbalanced they are likely to be, and the more likely they are to acci-dentally fall off a table, or windowsill (including outwards). Gifts from a shop, however, must be simple and straightforward. The sort of thing you'd buy for an estranged uncle (but not socks).

Cigarettes are a no-no, even if the doctor smokes like a lum[1]. I do remember the days of giving uncles and aunties cigarettes for Christmas, and the return-from-holiday present of a special big duty-free carton. But nowadays that's tantamount to assault – so fags are out. Oddly, sweeties and chocolates remain acceptable – even for fat doctors. I suppose it won't make them any fatter as they will inevitably have to 'share' these with the nurses and secretaries and, like 'Daddy's Easter Egg', they'll be polished off before the Doc is aware the box has been opened.

Alcohol is, I have to admit, my own fall-back position. Care is needed, since different alcohols have different connotations. A bottle of malt suggests you feel the doctor appreciates the better things in life, whereas a bottle of vodka or gin suggests you think he's a lush. Wine would be my choice – though you have to determine how knowledgeable the doctor is, plus factor in how much you yourself know, before making the appropriate choice. So here's a handy, unique, table. Each bottle will cost £8.62, but the effect will differ.

[1] Scottish for 'chimney', as in 'lang may yer lum reek.'

YOU KNOW	DOCTOR KNOWS	CHOICE
Lots	Lots	Little-known vineyard you came across on holiday (garnish it with a couple of the vine-leaves)
Lots	Medium	Portuguese red that you know is much better than one would think
Lots	None	Carefully chosen Chilean Malbec with a 2009 Leoville-Barton label pasted on.[2]
Medium	Lots	Second-cheapest medal-winning white from non-France in *Decanter*'s annual tasting
Medium	Medium	Vino Nobile de Montepulciano[3]
Medium	None	Mediocre Chateauneuf-du-Pape[4]
None	Lots	Malt Whisky Miniatures[5]
None	Medium	Any Australian Red with knitted Gnome on label and name like *Bastard Dingo Piss*
None	None	Cigarettes

[2] Genuine L-B 2009 should be kept > 15 years. He'll drink it now – so who could tell? If he does keep it, and eventually drink it in the company of expert, you'll be long gone.

[3] Very good, and he'll confuse it with *Brunello de Montalcino* – even better and much more expensive.

[4] Sounds good. Sounds French. He'll have heard of it. Expensive enough not to offend, the doctor will think it's much better than it actually is.

[5] If you go for the medal-winner, you'll mess it up and buy garbage.

CLOTHES

Seems silly, really.

Am I actually going to advise you on what clothes to wear when you visit your doctor? Well . . . yes. If Tranny and whatever-the-less-ugly-one-was-called could tell you (before Gok Wan presumably locked them in an abandoned wardrobe somewhere) what not-to-wear for a visit to the shops to buy . . . clothes, then it seems reasonable for me to make just a few suggestions. It *might* be important. And to work out what to wear, we look at the sort of things the doctor might be planning to do.

Taking your history

Don't wear any ill-fitting dentures.

Also worth avoiding are sparkling pieces of jewellery which might cause distraction. For females, this is particularly true for necklaces, amulets, fertility symbols or anything else tied around your neck basically to draw attention to your cleavage. Best not wear any cleavage at all. (For the sake of balance I should here also advise males seeing a female doctor not to distract her by wearing a nice smile, a kind personality, or a good-sense-of-humour.)

Things which you *should* wear to help the doctor take a history include the *well*-fitting dentures and a hearing-aid if you have one (by which I mean one that is yours and fitted for you because you need a hearing-aid – not if your sister Anne-Marie happens to keep your great-grandmother's in a sidedrawer of her old Welsh Dresser).

Examining you

The likelihood of this occurring is hugely variable. In my previous volume *Cynical Acumen*, I'd probably recount that your GP is extremely unlikely to examine you unless there's some sort of special deal that month with the local Health Board[1]. But I won't be saying such a thing here.

In hospital, the older a doctor is, the less likely he is to examine you – unless he is accompanied by a student or junior, whereupon he is forced to do all the stuff he ought to do but wouldn't normally cross his mind. Surgeons are more likely to examine you than physicians – though this examination will be scarily brief and limited to their specific area of interest, whereas a physician

[1] They have numerous keep-the-nation-healthy quotas they are obliged to meet. That's why your GP checks your blood pressure when you're up seeing about a bunion.

may carry out a 'general' examination. If a surgeon approaches you with a stethoscope, he's spotted an enormous spider behind your back.

How much clothing you need to remove will vary. Again, the older a practitioner is, the fewer clothes you will have to remove. Whilst hearing deteriorates in every other way imaginable as you get older, it magically becomes easier to listen to the lungs through a cardigan and two layers of shirt and vest (I do insist on moving any tie out of the way) after the age of forty. Again these magical abilities dissipate if a student is present, and the consultant who can normally identify an enlarged spleen with an index finger poked between a couple of jacket buttons will suddenly find himself removing the patient's shirt and even getting them to lie down nice and flat on the examining couch.

Loose-fitting garments may reduce the necessity for clothes removal, depending on the particular area under scrutiny. Thus floppy trousers may allow a practitioner to examine your knees with them simply pulled up. This is by no means ideal, but to be honest I find myself doing it more and more often – not through my normal laziness, more because of a bizarre local anti-infection ruling which has banned the use of cotton blankets over patients' legs in the clinics. The alternative throw-away gauze sheets are so redolent of translucent gossamer soft porn that most of us shy away from their use all together.

The ideal compromise is thus loose-fitting garments which are easily removed (bit like going to a night-club). Tight-fitting jeans, for example, are a disaster if the doctor plans to see more than two patients that day.

If asked to undress, do not feel embarrassed about NOT removing clothes you don't want to. This will not upset the doctor in the slightest. Some of us see it as a challenge (I planned an aside here 'unless it's something ridiculous like diagnosing a patient's gout without taking their shoes off' – but in fact that's dead easy. I just stand on their toes.) The doctor is more likely to be unsettled if you take off *more* than you have to. Lots of people don't want anyone to think they're embarrassed or prudish and once behind the screen rip off everything in double-quick time just to disprove this and show how supercool they are. Quite disconcerting to nip off for a tendon hammer and return to . . .

Top Tip No 9
Unless explicitly instructed otherwise, keep your pants on.

Taking your blood

Rule Number 1 is obvious. Nothing to do with how easy it is to roll up sleeves or anything like that. It's . . . *don't wear expensive clothes.* Mistakes do happen. And since we're trying to keep the doctor happy, we don't want them all upset that they've ruined your £2,000 Versace silk top. So . . . something inexpensive . . . dark colour . . . maybe deep red.

Loose-sleeved tops are certainly an advantage. And, for females, if you do ignore this advice and insist on some tight-sleeved arm-hugging number, then the trick is in what you wear under it. Make that . . . *something*, since you'll be taking the top off (and since blood-taking is now often done by a nurse or phlebotomist, doing so in a room or area where people don't usually take tops off, and passers-by may walk in casually to ask the time).

Checking Your Blood Pressure

If his quotas require it.
   Wear floppy sleeves.

Signing Your DLA Form

As with *Taking your blood*, avoid the £2,000 Versace silk top.
   Bring a pen.
   Not the Mont Blanc.

Top Tip No 10
The first time the medical team records your weight, don't take off your coat, boots, gold medallion etc. The second time, do take them off – that way it's easier to lose weight. (If attending the doctor for something where he wants you to gain weight, please reverse this advice).

GETTING YOUR OWN BACK

In a book purportedly designed to show you how to keep your doctor happy, it does seem a bit odd to have a chapter entitled 'getting your own back'. But in the immortal words of Ewan McGregor in Shallow Grave: 'You can't say you're not tempted!' And my plan is to perpetrate something of a cheat, and prompt you to take 'our' revenge on . . . medical students. This sticks to our original remit, since – as mentioned earlier – doctors themselves like to give students a bad time. If the patient seems to be joining in, that'll make us feel so much better about it, and about the world in general.

I have to admit that the techniques outlined below will work equally well on proper doctors. But since they're designed to ruin the practitioner's each and every attempt at examination and diagnosis, launching them at the guy who's actually trying to find out what's wrong with you and make it better it does rather smack of cutting off

your nose to spite your face.[1] The plan is to inter-
fere with students and doctors who are examining
you but not deciding your management. Obviously,
it'll be easier to sabotage what they're trying to
do if you have some idea what that is, so I'll take
you through the different areas of clinical examination and what the student doctor hopes to
achieve . . . and how we might make that less
likely.

Cardiovascular Examination ('The Heart')

First of all, the student will look at you to see if
you're breathless at rest. If you feel entirely well,
therefore, it might throw him off the scent to
breathe a bit faster, as if in some mild discomfort.
Alternatively, if you *are* dyspnoeic (our fancy
medical word for breathless), you might want to
fool him by breathing entirely normally – though
you may find this a bit trickier.

Next he'll want to take your pulse, normally at
the wrist. Only those trying to show off will use
the 'more accurate' carotid pulse in your neck –
whereupon affecting a faint (a 'feint'?) might
make him panic he's pressed a bit too hard. (He

---

[1] If you ever do cut off your nose to spite your face I'd
advise informing your plastic surgeon immediately, rather
than opting for a late presentation that will ruin his results
(as you mutter gleefully to yourself 'This'll make him
look bad.')

will be vaguely aware that you have two 'carotid sinuses' in the neck, closely attached to the carotid arteries. They respond to changes in pressure, and feed back information to the heart. Press one and your heart rate might drop. Press both and *you* might).

But back to the wrist. He'll first measure the rate, which stage you'll recognise as he fumbles with his watch – wishing he'd bought one with a second-hand. Students are usually taught to count the pulse over fifteen seconds and multiply by four, but the lack of a second-hand might explain any time-consuming (though extremely accurate) method of counting over five minutes and dividing by . . . five. For some reason, most of the dumb clucks find either of these mathematical manoeuvres hugely strenuous on the brain, and a simple murmuring – in a voice just loud enough – of random numbers . . . *fourteen . . . nineteen . . . twenty-one . . . twelve . . . fifteen . . . two . . .* will usually be enough to drive them bonkers.

Eventually he'll put away the timepiece (so you don't catch an infection) and move onto other aspects of the pulse he is obliged to assess. The main one is the 'rhythm' – specifically whether or not it is regular. One way to upset this apple-cart is to make use of 'sinus arrhythmia'. Everyone has this – to a variable extent. When you breathe in, your heart goes a bit faster – when you breathe out, a bit slower. Try it yourself. The younger you are, the more obvious it will usually be. So while your pulse is being assessed, try a gentle long breath-in, then out . . . then a few quick pants (trying not to make this too obvious). If the student announces that you have 'atrial fibrillation' then you've cracked it.[2]

After he's finished with your pulse he'll have a quick look at your hands. Various changes can occur here with various diseases, many of them to do with the heart, including a paleness of the creases of the palm that can happen with anaemia. This explains the sudden jump he'll then make to your eyes, seeing if the conjunctivae (that pinkish bit inside the lid) has the same pallor. In a medical exam situation, you could cause major trouble here if, no matter how careful and gentle he has been, you jump about as if your eye has been poked by a red-hot . . . poker. This is, however,

---

[2] Alternatively, you may have atrial fibrillation – less good news, but not miserable. The heart chambers usually pump blood in a nice sequence. Right atrium to right ventricle then out to lungs for oxygen. Back to the left atrium which pumps to left ventricle which pumps out to the body. Sometimes the atria start to 'fibrillate' in a useless wobble, and the ventricles pump randomly (if *they* just wobble, you're in real schtook) giving what we describe as an 'irregularly irregular' pulse. This is inefficient (but not disastrous). The main worry is that blood pooling around in the wobbly atria is prone to forming tiny clots, which the heart might scoot around your body ('emboli') to lodge in unfortunate places.

a bit extreme. And dangerous. If mistimed, its dubious authenticity may be obvious to an alert examiner. Whilst you may escape a yellow card for diving (or 'simulation', as both FIFA and GMC now term it), this will hinder your later efforts at causing havoc.

The next manoeuvre for the student is to look at the venous pulse in your neck, since this fills up if your heart is struggling (or 'failing' as we medics call it. While the lay public think 'heart failure' is a sudden-death-disaster thing [confusing it with 'cardiac arrest'] it's actually a long drawn-out problem with the heart 'failing' as a pump. Right-sided failure causes back pressure throughout the body with ankle-swelling [oedema] and stuff, while left-sided causes back pressure in the lungs [pulmonary oedema] with subsequent breathlessness, particularly when you lie down). You'll know he's about to do this 'Jugular Venous Pulse' when he starts mucking about with your pillows and seating position, as he's been taught that you should be at 45° for this. So if you can accidentally keep bouncing directly from 70° to 20° and vice-versa every time he adjusts you, it should drive him up the wall – though one limitation is that 95% of students have no idea what 45° looks like and will be entirely happy if you lie flat on your back.

When he fails to find the venous pulse in your neck (they always do. The JVP is the trickiest thing in all of medical examination technique) his next step is to press on your tummy over the liver, to push the pulse up. The blatant option here is to scream as though this is agonisingly painful. Better, just as he pushes on your tummy, is to breathe in sharply. This lets blood pool in the lungs, flattening out his attempted 'hepato-jugular reflux' and totally ruining the manoeuvre. And he won't notice.

Once he's bamboozled himself with the neck veins, the last move is on to examine the heart itself – or maybe just the chest wall over it. You may hear this called 'the precordium'. Now. We've warned you about this earlier. Particularly for the younger woman, it can be disconcerting as you take your top off and sit back in an unlikely relaxed fashion while he goes round to the foot of the bed and admires your funbags. In fact, he is looking for asymmetry (though advisedly not mentioning any if spotted), discolouration, pulses in the wrong places – that sort of thing. If you do suspect he is either taking too long or too many photographs, then you have an immediate chance to take revenge as he zones in, feeling for the 'apex beat' – the cardiac impulse usually felt under your left breast which can be pushed sideways if the heart is over-distended. Were you to surreptitiously move at precisely the right/wrong time such that your left nipple brushes against his hand, then react to this as if it was entirely the other way round, he would be in so-much-trouble.

However, I do not advise this.

a) Let's face it, this is a bit on the evil side of downright nasty.
b) If the move is spotted by the mentor/examiner, it will surely lead to an embarrassing red card, particularly after that earlier 'over the (eye)ball' incident.

The student then places the flat of his hand over each of the heart valve areas to see if he can feel the blood passing through any damaged valves. Normally he can't, but if he does it's called a 'thrill' – so there is that easy opening if he does say the 'feeling for thrills' line. Finally, he is allowed to pull out his stethoscope and listen to the quality of the two heart sounds (the 'lub-dup' caused by the closing of the valves) and for any murmurs (noisy flow over a tight or leaky valve). At this point I had considered suggesting that you might a) breathe out when he asks you to breathe in; b) breathe in when he asks you to breathe out; and c) wheeze as much as you possibly can while also telling him all the useful bits in your medical story which you didn't tell him earlier when he was actually wanting you to . . . when he asks you to '*hold your breath*'. But years of experience have taught me that you'll all do all of that anyway.

Respiratory Examination ('The Chest')

For some reason, examination of the lungs ('respiratory system') doesn't lend itself to creative

101

interference as much as the heart. Again the student will first look to see if you're breathless at rest with that admiring-your-breasts-manoeuvre, when a nice 'respiratory' touch to any feigned breathlessness might be to purse your lips when blowing out[3]. He will also be checking whether you have any 'cyanosis' – a bluish tinge in your tongue or lips (non-oxygenated haemoglobin!) associated with poorly functioning lungs – but we'll ignore this since it would be rather difficult to simulate if not present, or disguise if it were.

Hands will be examined for various changes in colour, temperature, nail-shape . . . basically lots of things outside your control. He'll look in your neck and armpits for lymph nodes. These are small nodules in the lymphatic system (cf. Glossary) that swell up when they're filtering infections or other inflammations (including . . . nasty things). Despite not secreting anything, they have always been referred to as 'glands' by the lay public, probably because they first come across them in the neck where they confuse them with swellings of genuine glands – the parotid and submandibular glands that produce saliva. The neck swelling in mumps

---

[3] Not advised for the same student who just examined your heart. Cardiac panting-like-a-dog while he examines the heart, then emphysematous forcing-the-air-out when he tries the lungs might make him smell a rat. But then, what's he doing walking down to the foot of the bed twice?

is the parotid – a genuine gland. The swellings in your neck when you get a Strep throat are lymph nodes, and arguably the most famous lymph nodes you have are your tonsils. This terming of lymph nodes as 'glands' has become so widespread that doctors have started to call them 'lymph glands' just to avoid a fight.

Next comes a look at your throat to make sure your windpipe is straight and in the midline. Not much you can do to muddy the waters here. Nor when he percusses (that tapping-thing) your chest. This test for fluid was devised around 1754 by one Auenbrugger, the smart-aleck medical-student son of a wine merchant/innkeeper. He watched dad's technique for seeing how much wine was left in the kegs and adapted it to diagnose pleural effusions (fluid around the outside of a lung – nothing to do with a 'barrel chest'). Sheer genius, and I'm sure it failed him a good bunch of exams. In reality, the student shouldn't be tapping your chest, but his own flattened finger ('pleximeter') from his other hand – but they usually miss. Unlikely to be painful barring huge fingernails, so you can't make much trouble there. However, when the stethoscope again rears its dangly head, one or two . . . opportunities appear with it.

It is possible to fake wheezy noises when you're breathing, but this is not advised. Fake wheezes are produced high up in the throat and are strikingly less obvious with the stethoscope than just listening with your ears – the exact opposite of the findings with *real* wheeze coming from the lungs. A good student may spot this. A more advanced approach is to pick one lung (or, more impressively, one area of one lung) and every time the student listens in that area, just breathe a bit less (whilst making the usual chest movements to cover this up). If consistently done, this area of 'reduced air entry' should fool him. It's less likely to fool any onlooking eminent examiner-type but you just might pull it off since most eminent examiner-types spend most eminent examining time asleep. Note this is a brilliant example of a technique *not* to be attempted with any doctors or other practitioners involved in actually looking after you. Otherwise you'll find yourself lying flat on your back having a tube the size of a garden hose rammed pointedly through your ribs before you can say 'how's your pneumothorax?'[4]

Recently a new opportunity has arisen to throw an exam candidate 'off the scent'. In the past,

---

[4] Cliché comic device, but doubly justified. A pneumothorax usually occurs when a bubble of air bursts *from* the lung into the 'potential space' between lung and chest-wall. The air expands to fill this 'vacuum' making the underlying lung collapse (pain!). The deceptive breathing outlined above will mimic the signs of this, prompting the insertion of chest-drain into *the space* to let the air out. But there isn't one. As it happens, the second way to get a pneumothorax is by letting in air from the *outside*, usually via the stabbing into *normal* lung of a sharp object like a dagger or . . . say . . . a chest drain.

it was always considered bad form for a candidate to learn the patient's diagnosis by any means other than taking the history and examination. The more blatant manoeuvres such as stealing case-notes or bribing an accompanying spouse are still, thankfully, frowned upon. But the surreptitious noting of medications on a locker or signs around the bed has somehow become acceptable, to the extent that this is now actively taught by commercial courses – *How-To-Pass-The-MRCP* and the like. Indeed a medical student I taught just this week told me she was searching around the bed because 'that will get me a point in the exam'. Know, therefore, that candidates will scan your surroundings for just such clues. So if you're *not* asthmatic, a borrowed inhaler poking out of your pyjama pocket might be a tasty manoeuvre – and easier than lugging in an oxygen cylinder. A carefully discarded BM stix for home sugar-testing may cause similar diversion, while if you can get your hands on a leaflet outlining *'How to Live with East-West Venezuelan Equine Encephalitis'* to tuck not-quite under your pillow . . .

Abdominal examination ('The Tummy')

It always surprises patients the first time they 'help with exams' (incidentally, an excellent way to keep your doctor happy). A freckle-faced kid is asked to 'examine the abdomen' and immediately grabs your hands, scrutinising the nails like an Amsterdam jeweller in *Hustle*. He then twists the hands round[5] and embarks on a lengthy analysis of the palmar markings as if deciding whether you're about to meet a tall dark stranger. There is an explanation. Particularly in an exam context, the hands are part of the examination of the abdomen. Candidates should have a quick look there for clues. For example, liver disease can cause white nails, fat nails ('clubbing' – lots of causes, including just being born with it . . . Hmmm . . . so if you *were* born with it, but pretend they just went that way in the last six months . . .), red palms, black bruises, lots of things. And they'll also be looking for those pale palmar creases of anaemia.

Eventually they get to the abdomen itself, and for this they will want you to lie fairly flat on your back as this relaxes the abdominal muscles and makes things like swollen organs easier to feel. You could cause trouble here by complaining this makes you breathless. This will render examination trickier, and perhaps as a bonus push their diagnostic cogitations towards unlikely causes of both chest and abdomen problems. However, I think our plan is to be awkward, but stop short of actually telling lies. (No, we *didn't* earlier. You

[5] Since most medical students assume this is the same as looking at the back label of a beer bottle, there's a 50–50 chance of this being in a painfully wrong direction.

weren't saying you were breathless, you were just . . . breathing more quickly than absolutely necessary)

They'll start with a gentle palpation over the whole abdomen. A few subtle winces here and there should slow them down, though this does unfairly punish the practitioner who cares about such things. If it is an exam, then it could be particularly devious to wince only when the student is not looking at your face (good once look up every now and again to see how you're doing). A good examiner should spot this ruse however, particularly in pantomime season.

After gentle palpation comes feeling for specifics . . . liver . . . spleen . . . kidneys . . . (the classic 'organ recital'). They get you to breathe heavily in-and-out to make the organs move up and down. For example, they will press their hand up towards your right ribs while getting you to breathe in, which pushes your liver edge (if the liver is enlarged) onto their hand. If you pretend that you think 'breathing in' is when you empty your chest (bringing it 'in') by pushing all the air out, then you'll muck up the whole examination. No-one will suspect a thing, since experience suggests that 78% of the population thinks in this way.

When they examine your testicles, scream at the top of your voice – but you don't really need me to tell you that.

Rheumatological and Neurological examination (joints and brain)

No tips.

None.

This is not because there are no opportunities to confuse the unsuspecting student, but because there are far too many. Examination of joints, muscles and nerves depends so much on the patient's co-operation that any amateur can make the doc's job impossible. *Yes that's sore, yes that's tender, no I can't move that leg up and no I didn't feel you touching that at all . . . or maybe actually it's a bit fuzzy . . . oh! When you touch that leg, I feel it in my other . . .*

For these systems, it's more fun to see it from the doctor's side, and try to find ways to catch *you* out. And I really can't divulge those here. I've already written an entire book for doctors with guidelines for spotting the truth amongst the persiflage – particularly the 'Cynical Tips' in a book entitled *Cynical Acumen* – and if I let you guys know these, the tips would be out-of-date.

Mind you, like the best of double-agents, I could then write *Cynical Acumen II* with ways of combating the knowledge that you guys now had . . . sell *that* to junior docs . . . and then I could . . . perhaps . . . maybe that would be *too* cynical.

The more perspicacious reader may suspect a

hidden agenda in this chapter. I'm wondering about it myself. Is it all cod psychology in action? It's well known that you shouldn't tell children what not to do. They'll immediately want to test this out and see what happens when they do. Thus, you don't tell your child *not* to walk on the road, you tell him/her *to walk* on the pavement. Don't tell them not to eat with dirty fingers, tell them to wash their hands before eating. Apparently it makes a difference. So when I realised there were a lot of really annoying things that patients do when you're examining them that I'd really like to tell them NOT TO, did I instead list all the things that you could do to upset the doctor, tarting it up with some story about upsetting students, hoping this would then make you avoid them if you indeed 'want to keep your doctor happy'? And just maybe this helps everybody, as happy doctors make better doctors, and better doctors make patients better.

I simply don't know.

Must ask my psychologist.

DON'T MENTION THE WARD

Things Not to Say in the Consulting Room

Top Ten things *not* to mention when visiting the doctor.

1 The Internet

You know the sort of thing.

'I've been reading up on my diagnosis on the Internet, Doctor, and don't you think it might be better if . . .?'

This is clearly going to cause trouble, regardless of whether the Internet is wrong, irrelevant, or (worst-case scenario) hits the nail squarely on the head. This isn't because doctors are high-handed characters with a God Complex who think they know everything. That's just a coincidence[1]. Even your nice doctor who knows he can be wrong, knows he can make mistakes – who certainly knows that he cannot be *au fait* with every recent advance in every disease in the

---

[1] In fact, not even true. This generalisation much loved by the Press and disgruntled relatives (of patients, not of the Press) describes only a tiny subset of doctors – known as surgeons q.v.

medical dictionary – might well be unsettled by your playing the Internet card. They don't want to be treated as some omniscient being, demanding deference from all and sundry. But they do want the same courtesy you would show anyone else. If the plumber comes round and says that your central heating needs a new valve, you wouldn't tell him that you've been reading up on the Net and *doyouwantblockedpipesthiswinter.com* says that any time your central heating stops working, there's *no point* in changing a valve and you should go straight on to fitting a new 8X581F pump and that'll fix the whole thing. The plumber might find that a bit presumptuous, and reasonably ask 'why call me in the first place?'[2]

---

[2] See? The plumber analogy is a winner. It *proves* you guys are awkward, calling in docs you don't need . . . except . . . you do need us to *prescribe drugs*. Rats! All my analogies might be unfair. OK, let's rewind. Areas where I complain we're treated worse than tradesmen. 1) Patients come along with trivial problems – equivalent to a flat tyre or leaky washer that people would fix for themselves. 2) Patients 'second-guess' the doctor's performance like they wouldn't with mechanic/plumber unless they were one themselves. However, both behaviours are foisted upon them because they can't buy drugs. They're forced to seek the doctor's help when otherwise they mightn't have bothered. And having being forced against their will, it's reasonable to take a jaundiced view of what the 'authorised' quack is up to . . . This is a disaster!! Years of my justified complaining shown to be unjustified. Must acknowledge this . . . but not broadcast it too widely. Maybe if I hide it in a footnote . . .

Doctors are the same. They don't think they know everything, but do sort-of assume there's a fair chance they'll know more medicine than you. Nobody would suggest you can spend five years at University and learn nothing at all, unless it's in America (or OxBridge and they went to the other one).

So don't give them stupid amounts of respect. Just the normal for any tradesman or professional you'd gone to see with a problem, rather than assuming a night on the Net makes you an expert. The Net is, after all, the last great uncensored medium. You can write anything on it, and nobody can stop you. Even pornography usually causes trouble only for the people downloading it, while the guys putting it up there get away Scot-free. So if you use a drug on 2,000,000 people and three of them get better, no-one can stop you advertising on the Net, telling everybody about the three successes, never mentioning the other 1,999,997 that all went bald.

You can't assume that everything you read on the Net is true, since even the most apparently balanced site may have a hidden agenda. So if you've read about some drug which entirely eradicated diabetes from Arkansas, USA, just ask your doc if he's heard of it, rather than demanding 200mg twice daily just in case you were about to develop diabetes sometime next year.

Which brings us to . . .

2 Drugs they are using in America

This upsets most UK doctors, not just because of inherent nationalistic sensitivities (though every doctor in every country of every world thinks their own medics are the best, and would spend a fortune flying a family-member home rather than trust the local quacks. Of course, most have prejudices against all things foreign, leading to major dilemmas e.g. in choosing between a Moscow gynaecologist and an urgent trip home on *Aeroflot . . .*) but also because of its historical making-no-sense-at-all. All down to the FDA. The Food and Drugs Authority – the USA regulatory body to which all companies must submit tons of evidence to prove their new product both works and isn't stupidly dangerous (it's not clear how hamburgers got through). For years the FDA has been more stringent than the equivalent European bodies with its criteria for allowing drugs to be 'licensed'. Presumably this is an avoiding-litigation thing and not an over-riding imperative-not-to-harm-anyone lying dormant or otherwise well-disguised in the American psyche. Traditionally, therefore, most drugs have become available in the UK before the US. Over the years, a number of my patients have insisted on trying the new wonder-drug that they'd read was sweeping America only to face major disappointment when I told them it was the same one they had been taking for the past eighteen months.[3] Their disbelief is understandable, since Press reports for the USA 'breakthrough' will usually bear no resemblance to their own experience of the drug. This may simply relate to the USA's universal enthusiasm for everything new, but could reflect a tendency to emphasise a drug's brilliance in the eyes of a patient who is more directly having to pay for it.

Things have changed recently. Although drugs are still promptly licensed in the UK, there's now a delay while different authorities/committees (*NICE* – National Institute of Clinical Excellence – in UK; *SMC* – Scottish Medicines Consortium – in Scotland[4]) decide if the drug works well enough to justify its price to the NHS. Value and side-effects are thus analysed along with its efficacy. So nowadays drugs may become available in the US before the UK, since as far as I know the FDA only has to convince itself

---

[3] Often doing very well on it too. It's an odd phenomenon that some patients are ultra-keen to try new drugs, even when the old ones are working fine.

[4] I hear you. Scotland is *in* the UK (at the time of writing). However (ditto.), the SMC decides within months of a drug's launch whether it is 'accepted for use' by the NHS in Scotland. This is the *status quo* until NICE makes its decision for the entire UK about 2–4 years later (if ever). Scotland just happens to be miles ahead of England. Personally I think the Sassenachs are distracted by all that repeated participation in the football World Cup. And we . . . aren't.

that the drug is safe – and let *you* worry about the price.

I think an aside is required here, too long for even one of my footnotes. I am clearly describing some sort of rationing of drug usage in the UK. How does that sit with the NHS ideal of best possible care being made available to everyone for 'free'? If a drug works, surely you should get it, no matter how much it costs? Is it possible, ever, to justify not using a drug simply because it's too expensive? Can we put a price-tag on someone's life? Or 'quality of life'?

Of course not.

Or at least, such was my own view, held for years, until the practicalities eventually wore me down, and I told myself this:

First, realise that not all the money in the world is available to the NHS.

Then:

Say you invented a drug which could be absolutely proven to make everyone with lung cancer live *one* more day – no side-effects – and it cost £1. Would you give it to everyone with cancer? *Clearly, yes.*

What if it cost £10? *Yes.*

What if it cost £100? . . . *erm* . . . *Yes.*

£1,000? . . . *erm* . . .

£1,000,000? . . . *erm* . . . *No.*

If you still think it doesn't matter what the price is, go back to the non-infinite resources concept. Plus don't think of it as the country spending money, but yourself – or your loved ones. And ask yourself... would *you* give away £1,000,000... £100,000 ... £1,000 of your children's inheritance so that you could live one more day?

So, like it or not, we must admit there does come a point, a cost, at which it just isn't . . . 'right'.

And what if it only gives one person in ten the extra day (and you don't know who) . . .?

And what if it *does* cause side-effects (and you don't know who) . . .?

In the end, authorities have been forced to come up with ways to assess all these things to ensure some degree of value-for-money with the drugs they buy. And you can't really blame them.

Most of the ways relate to a use of the 'QALY' concept. Quality-Adjusted-Life-Years. If a drug made you live for an extra year and you felt absolutely well, then that drug would give you an extra QALY. If it cost £10,000, that would be £10,000 per QALY. If it only made you live for six months, that would be £20,000 per QALY. If it kept you alive and in perfect health as long as you took it and it cost £10,000 per year – that would also be £10,000 per QALY. All fairly straightforward. But what if it keeps you alive, but you still have the disease and feel ill, or can't walk (or are unconscious all day), or the drug itself gives you a side-effect, like nausea? Then we have quite tricky (and impossible to validate) techniques of estimating the quality of your life compared with normality . . . or is it with perfection? If I'm not living the life of

116

David Beckham, am I missing out on something? A thing called a 'Utility Value' for your life has been devised – so if you are entirely well, it's 1.0 (even if you're not fit enough to play for England). If you're too breathless to get out of the house, but are still alive, mobile and *compos mentis*, this might give your life a Utility Value of, say, 0.5. Keeping you alive at that level had better cost half-as-much as keeping a well person going . . .

Gauging the Utility Value somebody 'is left with' when afflicted by a serious illness is unachievable, but creative attempts are made. One method is the 'gambling technique' where a large group of people are asked how many years of their life they would give up NOT to have a particular affliction. So if a thirty-five-year-old might be expected to have another forty years in her, how many of those would she give up to have her blindness cured[5]? Sounds far-fetched, unpalatable even – but this technique is the gold standard. Other methods can produce bizarre comparisons in scale – particularly if a drug company is cherry-picking data that suits a drug 'submission' to a regulatory body. It wouldn't do to take these massaged data to heart, otherwise a recent example with a 'utility value' for life on

---

[5] My daughters both agreed they would give up seven years not to have facial hair (if they had it!). Since they had theoretically 55 years to play with, that means facial hair drops your Utility Score by 0.13. It was a genuine question, re a genuine drug.

chemotherapy after an operation for brain tumour just *bettering* that of a well adult who is sadly *over fifty years old* might have upset me even more . . .

It's all a bit impossible. But the powers-that-be have to come up with some sort of plan to decide how to spend the available money.

Which again nicely brings us to . . .

3 A Drug That Your Doctor Should Be Giving You But Isn't Because it's too Expensive

Doctors find the merest hint of this suggestion extremely upsetting. There's clearly an insult somewhere in there, but where? Is the doctor incompetent . . . or uncaring . . . or is it his beloved NHS that doesn't care and he doesn't have the guts to stand up for his patient and do the right thing? The multiple-insult-complex is particularly irritating because he knows the truth boils down to three possibilities:

i) The drug is simply not indicated for the patient's condition. To use rheumatology as an example and to use yesterday (honest) to show how topical and real this example is, a patient with clear-cut osteoarthritis/ degenerative arthritis/wear-and-tear-in-the-joints[6]

[6] A campaign outlining these three diagnoses as synonymous would make my life so much easier.

took great umbrage that I wasn't going to give him the new AntiTNF/mono-clonal antibody/magic bullet/Biologics[7] at £10,000 a pop (actually per year, but that might make it sound a potential bargain). These drugs simply will not work at all in osteoarthritis. It would be like giving toxic vomit-inducing, hair-losing, marrow-blasting anti-cancer therapy for a wart.

ii) The drug is one where the risk of side-effects isn't justified by the severity of the patient's condition. Again I refer to arthritis. Anti-TNF drugs are not only expensive, they're also potentially toxic. They are also new, and may have extra toxicities we don't suspect (and we already suspect a lot). So you won't use them on mild rheumatoid arthritis already controlled by other drugs – even though they *will*, in this case, help. There is a set of criteria to justify the use of these drugs depending on disease severity, which, because of potential toxicity, we might still largely follow even if they cost thruppence.

iii) The drug is indeed a drug-that-your-doctor-should-be-giving-you-but-isn't-because-it's-too-dear. As with the Internet-actually-

[7] Whereas everybody seems to know these are synony-mous. Maybe the Net should help with *simple* things.

telling-the-truth possibility mentioned above, this is the most irritating for the doctor. When the patient is right on the money . . .

4 Football

Unless you have time on your hands and you're the last patient. Maybe it's just me, but I'll happily talk about last night's game until the cows come home. The next patient in the queue might not be so understanding.

5 The last letter 'I' sent your GP

Always assuming you are mentioning it to complain about something it said and not congratulate me on the pretty stamp.

First off, don't say 'the letter you sent' if it wasn't me. I refuse to take responsibility for every letter sent to every patient by every doctor, secretary, records manager in the hospital.

Second off, don't complain about something I *did* write about you if you plan to remain my patient. In the short term, you get the satisfaction of being 'one-up', but in the long term you jeopardise communication between myself and your GP. Whilst we doctors are well aware that patients can now see everything we write about them, we put this squarely to the back of our minds and work in a pretend world (once called 1978) where doctor-doctor correspondence is sacrosanct and we can say what we really think. For example, patients take great exception if we think there's 'nothing wrong with them', so we almost never say that to them. If a patient tells me a doctor said there was nothing wrong them, I usually assume that the doctor didn't make the diagnosis the patient wanted/expected and they remember this as the doctor saying there was nothing wrong with them because . . . they themselves knew there was nothing wrong with them (and will often take umbrage at the unvoiced statement). In discussions with such patient, we are more likely to make reassuring noises with vague non-scary diagnostic possibilities – while we arrange investigations to ensure that nothing is indeed wrong with them. We will not tell you that we're doing a test to exclude the 1:1,000 chance of cancer or arthritis, but we will do the test. We should let the GP know that while we are doing these tests, we do not think for a moment that any of them will be positive. But if you read this letter and get upset because I think there's nothing wrong or because I'm checking for cancer without telling you – or even complain about both – then my future letters to your GP will go all vague and fuzzy . . . and basically I'll stop telling your GP the actual truth.

Of course it is reasonable to correct factual inaccuracies. If I tell the your GP it's all down to stress because you're having an affair with your wife's sister, and what you'd actually told me was that you'd gone to the fair with your wife and sister, then I'm happy to set the record straight.

6 (Asking for) The results of your tests

We doctors like to think that the diagnostic process isn't just about Xrays or blood results. No. It's an intricate and subtle jigsaw constructed from the patient's story, their past history, the findings on examination *and* the test results. These we put together using years of experience, expertise, clinical acumen and all-round genius, and come up with a working diagnosis. To ask for 'the results of the tests' is such an insult – and reminds us that all of the above is a delusion. This will occasionally provoke someone like myself into 'nippy' mode.

'So, I want to know the results of all of my blood tests.'

'Well, your haemoglobin was one-hundred-and-thirty-two grams per litre, the White Cell Count was 5,400 per cubic millimetre, and the MCV was 96 femtolitres[8].'

'What does that m- . . . .? . . . I don't know what any of that means!'

'So why did you ask?'

Tremendously grumpy, I know, but would you really ask the guy doing your car's MOT for the readings on the exhaust chemistry, rather than

---

[8] Femtolitre. A personal favourite. It's a thousandth millionth millionth of a litre – and it's used to measure the size of individual red cells.

accepting the simple news that they're fine? ('*The hydrocarbons were what?!? Have you checked the EGR valve?*') Most doctors will tell you precise results if they think it will be of some help to do so. Otherwise they won't. Sounds paternalistic, but it's not so much that what you don't know won't hurt you, as what you don't know that we don't know won't worry you unnecessarily. There's no point in giving you the details of every red herring that flies across the meandering path to the diagnosis.

It's particularly unsettling when relatives demand to know the current thinking, based on results so far. Until a final diagnosis is reached, little is gained by sharing the numerous possibilities – good and bad – with relatives. They always want to know the most likely diagnosis at any moment in time. What is the point of that? It almost always changes. Any doctor spouting his current thoughts is asking for trouble when later they turn out to be 'wrong' and he looks like a tube. The oftheard complaint that doctors 'won't tell us anything except that they're still doing tests' is really a complaint that 'that doctor isn't stupid enough to put himself forward for ridicule.' You won't get Alan Hansen to predict a result just so you can shoot him down later, so why expect the doctor to do it? If doctors are still doing tests, it's because they don't know the answers . . . what useful information can you get from them except precisely that?

Note that this refers to the occasions when you are face to face with the doctor – when you can see that he does himself have all the results. When you've gone and attended for some specific test and have heard no word, it's a good idea to call up about it – amongst other things making sure that the result has indeed got back to your doctor.

7 'Blah-de-blah blah.' 'oh, and bleh-de-bleh bleh' 'and I forgot rhubarb . . . rhubarb . . .' . . . basically anything *while the doctor is taking blood.*

'Venepuncture' is normally a simple procedure. Nice plump vein you can feel easily . . . stick needle in . . . bingo!

But you should be aware of the signs that all's not going so well . . . the doctor tries the tourniquet on the other arm . . . he tries a different tourniquet . . . starts gently slapping your antecubital fossa (that's the bit on the front of your elbow where we take blood from) . . . frowns . . . breathes a bit heavier . . . slaps your hand harder – like he *means it* this time . . . gets a bit sweaty . . . asks you to clench and unclench your fist . . . goes back to the first arm again . . . starts to look at the veins on the back of your hand . . . or the side of your neck . . . watches your arm change colour . . .

When you spot this happening . . . SHUT THE £$%&%^* UP! You are leaning over the shoulder of someone who's soldering a micro-chip . . .

124

painting a portrait . . . chopping tiny vegetables . . . fixing a watch . . . threading a needle – and it ain't going according to plan. They don't want you *talking to them*.

Some phrases to avoid:

i) '*They never usually have a problem with me – I'm dead easy to get blood from.*' Much more appreciated is the psychologically-aware patient who says 'oh, they always have trouble – my veins are rubbish!'

ii) '. . . Dracula! . . .' If all the patients who ever came out with this original witticism were laid end-to-end . . . it'd be me that put them there.[9]

iii) '*A little blood . . . that's nearly an armful! . . . heh Doc, did you ever see the Tony Hanc-?*'

Yes I have seen it, despite its being thoroughly before my time. Good, if dated. But I could never work out why the bit about the 'armful' of blood has been remembered by a generation-and-a-half of people as being in some way either humorous or witty.

8 I hardly eat a thing all day

It's a given in medical circles. All fat patients hardly eat a thing. It's their metabolism, doc.

I've already called upon the Universal Laws of

[9] With apologies to Dorothy Parker.

Physics to pronounce this as tosh – so I shouldn't really have to mention today's newspaper story of the man who had tried everything (weight-watchers, calorie-counting, gym, specialists, herbals, homoeopathy . . .) to lose weight, but is finally shedding pounds and pounds after treatment by hypnosis . . . which the paper fails to emphasise clearly works because it makes him *eat less*.

But I will.

Case proven, m'Lud..

9 The University of Life

Patients often lay great store by what they have learned from The University of Life. The phrase itself is somewhat dated, and will only be quoted in direct repudiation if the doctor blunders into suggesting his own university gives him the upper-hand in the knowledge stakes. More common now is the 'I know my own body' approach. Presumably the implication is that having the disease gives you innate knowledge of its diagnosis and treatment. While I am happy with my usual defence to this – that most people with tuberculosis would prefer to be treated by someone who'd read a bit about tuberculosis, rather than someone who'd *had* tuberculosis – it usually falls on deaf ears since The University of Life almost exclusively crops up when seeing patients with nothing wrong with them in the first place. Give them tuberculosis[10] and they'll soon change their tune.

10 Doctors' being overpaid

This used to upset doctors because we were bitter about being paid a pittance for overtime (genuinely . . . it was 35p per hour) and nothing at all for on-call. We viewed ourselves as *underpaid* with respect to other professionals, workers 'in the City', entertainers and footballers. How come nobody resented the artist formerly known as Posh Spice earning 200 times more than I did? Yet, since our underpaidness was not with respect to the patient themself, we couldn't really adopt that stance.

Then came the New Contract of the mid-2000s. It means we get paid for working late, or at weekends, or overnight, and our pay has risen until . . . we probably *are* being overpaid. So now we find the *accurate* accusation is even more upsetting, and totally indefensible (though I still think Simon Cowell has the edge. He does, after all, in one month earn three times what I will earn in my entire lifetime).

[10] Hypothetically speaking. This isn't a punishment exercise.

DON'T MUNCH IN THE WARD

Things Not to Do in the Consulting Room

1 Over-embellish symptoms

We all want people to realise when we are in pain. This we learn as children. Mummy will hug us and make us feel better, so at the first hint of discomfort we let her know all about it in no uncertain terms. Forty years on, we all want the doctor to take our symptoms as seriously, even though a hug is usually out of the question. But what you must avoid is any over-exhuberance in describing your symptoms in an ill-advised attempt to impress him with the extent of your problem. It may have entirely the opposite effect. The doctor spends his entire life seeing lots of people with lots of diseases. He knows how much pain, discomfort, upset, they tend to cause. If you describe a pain outwith the normal limits, either you have some bizarre version of the disease he hasn't seen before, some totally different disease he hasn't seen before . . . or you're exaggerating the symptoms. And if you are exaggerating . . . who's to say you aren't making it all up in the first place?

That's the rule in any court-room drama I've ever seen. If you say the defendant attacked you with a knife while you were having steak and chips, and the defending lawyer can prove you had chicken and chips, the game's over. Once you're caught out in one lie, no matter what, your whole testimony goes down the plughole. Of course exaggeration isn't telling lies, but it's well recognised when reviewing GP referral letters to rheumatology clinics that if the GP says the patient is 'complaining bitterly' of pain, you don't rush to put them on the 'Urgent' list. So just tell it as it is, and leave the doctor to use his experience to work out what that means[1]. Your mum will give you a hug no matter how thick you lay it on, but as we've already agreed, the doctor does NOT love you as much as your mummy does.

2 Over-embellish signs[2]

Again, the doctor knows what degree of discomfort or pain to expect during examination either pressing bits or putting other bits through various manoeuvres. The opportunity to cause pain is, after all, the reason many of us became doctors (we hide it better than dentists). If the patient is

[1] The corollary of this is: if you *are* sore, breathless or fatigued, say so. Being reticent, stoical, or just plain butch is also no help in getting to the right diagnosis.
[2] A symptom is something you complain of; a sign is something the doctor finds on examination.

grimacing and wincing throughout the examination when we're not even *trying* to hurt them, we'll likely take this with a huge pinch of salt. No need to worry if you *are* making it all up – as we'll both know where we stand – but if you're just trying to over-emphasise real pains, I might fail to see the wood for the trees. I have been forced to explain this badly to patients, since someone writhing in agony as if they had a perforated ulcer when you're gently examining their abdomen has to be stopped somehow, so you can discover anything subtle underneath this. The alternative – to operate on them for a non-existent perforated ulcer – would seem a rather harsh lesson on crying wolf.[3]

3 Re-iterate information once we've 'moved on'

I'm being harsh here. But it really is no help at all, having already been informed that the patient's knee is painful walking, going up stairs, going down stairs (in genuine cases usually the worse of the two, but I'm not going to let you know that), cycling, dancing, getting into the car, getting out of the car . . . to be told whilst listening to tricky heart sounds through the stethoscope that it's also sore climbing onto a bus. That info isn't going to

---

[3] Technically, the lesson on crying wolf would be to wait for them to have a perforated ulcer and not operate, but you know what I mean.

make or break the diagnosis. But it might make the doctor miss a subtle diastolic murmur, or in my case a blatant one.

In general, once the doctor starts examining you, don't add anything to the history unless it's crucially important. This does NOT include that it's 'also sore when I'm climbing mountains', or that 'it's a different pain from the one my brother had', though maybe 'Cheeeez . . . your hands are cold!'

I should add that this refers to hospital visits, where the consultation usually goes through three distinct phases. In the GP surgery, the advice is more difficult to follow. History-taking will overlap examination and even the writing of the prescription . . . indeed it may not necessarily be obvious which came first.

4 Mention another symptom just as you're leaving

Irritating in the extreme.

I've gone into the story of your painful knees, all the different times when they're most sorest, which buses are the worst to climb onto, got your clothes off, examined you . . . thoroughly . . . moving all of the joints around . . . come to the diagnosis of osteoarthritis (is this boy good or what?), got your clothes back on again, taken some blood tests just to make sure it's nothing else, chatted to you about the diagnosis, what you can do about it . . . lose weight, exercise, wear trainers, go swimming, maybe take these tablets . . . discussed the comparative merits of Yoga and Tai Chi . . .

Then, just as you reach the door and I'm waving goodbye whilst surreptitiously eyeing the next patient's case sheet, you say, 'and is that what's making me cough up blood?'

5 Take a Call on Your Mobile

Other than to say you'll call back. If you do start a conversation, don't be surprised if I lean forward and make obvious efforts to eavesdrop. I also do this on trains, since I think anyone who insists on disturbing folk with their private conversations has given up all rights to their being private.

Please note this has nothing to do with any ideas of your mobile interfering with the workings of essential life-saving machinery. That whole concept is clearly bollocks – same as in aeroplanes. Think about it. If your chirruping mobile really could send your 747 plummeting into a mountain, do you think they would let you *anywhere near* the plane with it? Of course they would. Like it's perfectly safe to trust absolutely everybody to switch off when the jaunty stewardess casually mentions it after demonstrating how to whistle up someone to pull you out of the Atlantic? I don't think so.

If it were true, terrorists would realise there's a much easier plan than stuffing 99mls of explosive cocktail into six separate pairs of trainers . . . and simply turn their mobiles on . . .

No.

It's just plain rude.

6 Eat a sandwich

Unless you're a diabetic in desperate need of bringing up your blood sugar (in which case . . . sugar would be my choice – and try not to bring it up), eating whilst seeing the doctor is just as rude as at any other meeting not involving close friends, family, and a dinner table.

7 Drink Coke

Snorting it is arguably worse.

8 Confuse your hospital consultant with your GP

This usually happens in clinics dealing with chronic illnesses such as arthritis and diabetes. Patients get used to regular visits, probably seeing the hospital doctors more often than their family doctor, and begin to regard it as a regular check-up. They then hang onto symptoms they've developed and don't see their GP about them because they've got a diabetes clinic appointment in a month or so. Just today (genuinely) one of my patients told me she had poked a stick into her left eye a month back and it was still irritating her, and did I think maybe . . .?

This isn't that unusual, and the trouble is not that I'm far too busy and important to bother doing the 'menial' work of a GP[4] (I am, after all, only a rheumatologist), it's more that . . . well . . . I won't know anything about it, and embarrassingly will have to refer this back to said General Practitioner, much reducing my street-cred in the irritated eyes of Mrs Smith. More worryingly, the patient may have left an important symptom to fester for an unnecessary six weeks.

9 Make a List

It's one of the world's great paradoxes. The doctor says he wants you to be precise. Did the headache start before or after the fall? Had the GP already prescribed the antibiotic before the rash began? Just when *did* you post the cheque? . . .

Clearly it would be a good idea in the midst of all this stress to have the details at your fingertips, and the obvious answer is to . . . write a list.

WRONG!

The moment a doctor sees that you've made a list of all your symptoms and when they happened and what the GP did about them he'll immediately mark you down as a neurotic. From then on everything is downhill (in the bad sense – I realise it's

[4] So, I *don't* compare it to a defendant walking into the courtroom with the QC who's trying to get him off a bang-to-rights armed-robbery charge. He taps said QC on the shoulder: 'Oh – another thing. I was wondering if you could help me get a mortgage?'

tricky because 'uphill' is also bad). He'll not believe a word of it.

Best plan, therefore, is indeed to possess a list/time-line of everything that's happened, but not let the doctor get so much as a glimpse of its physical form. Memorising the details is best – though silently mouthing the intervening words to get to the relevant point might look suspicious, or worse. Don't get caught consulting any 'cribs' as this would be more damaging than admitting to the list in the first place.

10 Assume Doctors recognise tablets by their colour

And how much of the methotrexate are you taking?

Sixteen per day.

Sixteen? That's a lot. Particularly since you're only supposed to take them once a week.

Are they no the white wans?

I don't think so . . . not usually . . . though I tend to distinguish drugs by their names rather than –

Must be those big yins then – I take them on Wednesdays.

And how many do you take?

Three . . . naw! . . . eight.

So which is it, three or eight?

Dunno. I think . . . five, maybe.

And what dose?

Fifty millimetres.

. . . you get tens and two-and-a-halfs . . .

. . . two-and-a-halfs, then . . . oh, I don't know. Have ye no got it written down there somewhere?

Well, we've got written down how many we want you to take and how many we think you are taking, but –

Aw ah don't bother with all that stuff. I'm aye getting' mixed up. My wife looks after it all, puts them in one o' them box-things . . .

Dosette boxes. Fair enough. But since it's your body, you should really take some interest in the drugs that you are taking.

Nae chance. I've never any idea even what time of day it is – what wi' the jet lag and stuff.

Jet lag?

Yeah. I'm a pilot with GlobWorld Airways.

. . . You've never mentioned that.

Nope. If I mention I'm an airline pilot, you'll never let me have rheumatoid arthritis . . . naw . . . wait . . . that should be the ither way round.

. . . OK . . . we'll leave that and get you . . . wait! I should really ask – what are the sixteen white tablets you're taking every day?

I dunno . . . maybe I'm getting mixed up . . . maybe it's the wife that takes them . . .

PHRASES THAT SAY YOU'RE MAKING IT UP

I'm not sure I should be telling you this.

It takes most doctors a large part of their formative years to accumulate clues, hints and downright giveaways that let them know (like a poker player's 'tells') the patient in front of them is making up a story, pushing the doctor to come to a diagnosis that is not necessarily correct. There are a number of reasons why this takes so long. Firstly, it will be some time before the neonate medic realises that any patient would ever do such a thing. It is, after all, a secret which has been kept sternly from him throughout his training. The Medical Establishment[1], wanting to 'keep in' with the media, patient-groups and other 'good people' (that's how you get to remain an Establishment) clings to the dictum that all patients tell the truth, and no-one ever 'kids on', and this is therefore taught to students.

[1] The GMC, Royal Colleges, BMA and the like, whose high-heid-yins are forever giving 'The doctors' view' in the Press but whose opinions no more represent those of real doctors than . . . mine do.

The idea that some people might welcome a spurious diagnosis as this a) gets them off work, b) gets them compensation, c) gets them a benefit payment or early retirement d) gets them a niche in their family/social order where they gain sympathy, affection or even physical aid, e) gets them drugs etc. is anathema to the Medical Establishment. I assume that individually they must at least entertain this possibility which is taken for granted by the rank and file of *real* doctors, but no-one wants to put their head above the parapet and suffer the opprobrium of the pressure groups. Why lose the Knighthood for nothing?

So it's already some time before the young doctor even suspects that all may not always be what it seems. Once aware, he must also devise his own techniques for spotting when he is being taken-for-a-ride. No-one will tell him, as that would break the unwritten code.

OK. Having upset every Establishment doctor in the land (not to mention most right-thinking humans) by suggesting that some patients are putting it on, I now propose to upset the other doctors by telling all you potential scam-merchants out there the things to avoid saying if you don't want to give the game away. I have two defences. One is that these giveaways are not absolute. Some people with genuine problems will of course use them innocently. So by letting all of you, my genuine (gentle) readers know what they are, I simply help you avoid giving the wrong impression to a cynical medic. The other defence is that these are the clues utilised by *me*; they are biased towards rheumatology and will no way be an exhaustive list of the available pointers. Other doctors probably have their own.

Besides.

I *like* upsetting people.

1 'You tell me, you're the doctor . . .'
This piece of aggressive defensiveness can occur very early in the consultation, where the patient sets the tone:

'Hello, Mr Smith, sit down . . . so what is it that's been troubling you?'
'You tell me. You're the doctor.'

But is more commonly encountered at a later stage, e.g. when the doctor is trying to clarify some detail in the history which doesn't quite make sense:

'So if they thought it was your gall bladder causing the problem, why was it they took out your spleen?'
'You tell me. You're the doctor.'

Or:

'So if the pains only started on Thursday, why were you already prescribed tablets for them on Tuesday?'
'You tell me, you're the doctor.'

Patients don't realise that this line is a sure sign they have a 'hidden agenda'. Perhaps you don't believe this and you think it's an over-interpretation on my part. So let's go to the other time you'll find a similar phrase used – and it's not at the garage.

A *'It wasn't me.'* . . .
. . . *'Who do you think organised it?'*
'You're the detective.'

or

B *'So how do you explain all that blood we found in the car?*
'You tell me, you're the detective.'[2]

You see? This line is not for the doctor-patient relationship. This line is the sort of thing a police suspect says. It's confrontational, avoids the question, and suggests the suspect realises he has no good answer. The investigator's logic catches him out and he has nowhere to go. So when a patient rushes to adopt this pose, what are we supposed to think . . .?

2 'You're confusing me with all your questions.' Or 'I'm all confused with all these questions.'
This phrase also smacks of the interrogation room.

[2] A. *A Small Death in Lisbon:* Robert Wilson. B. *CSI:* whenever.

It is most likely to occur in the A&E department rather than GP consultation, when a hospital bed for the night may be preferable to the patient's alternatives[3] (maybe a night on the street, a night in the jail, or a night in the doghouse following a post-midnight domestic confrontation . . .). A follow-up with the cop-procedural 'I've already been through all of this with the other doctor (*your sergeant*)' is a clincher. All genuine patients are happy to tell their story as many times as it takes for someone to get the diagnosis right. Non-genuines don't really like repeating their story – aware of the implications if it's not the same one.

I must admit here that there is a universally accepted argument against my distrust of the 'I'm all confused' stance – namely that the stress of being ill will confuse patients and give them a changeable story. My own theory is that a story is usually changeable only because when 'under pressure' you don't have the truth to fall back on.

3 'And sometimes it gives way . . .'

Spookily enough, a major 'giveaway'.

Usually concerning a joint (but sometimes an entire limb), and most usually the knee. This phrase is used to impress the doctor that there is

[3] I'm with you, pedant. I hate using 'alternative' when there are more than two possibilities – but 'options' just seemed overoptimistic for someone in this predicament.

some *major* problem in the joint. But it's too impressive. The level-of-problem such that the joint will genuinely give way is so huge that it'll be wobbling about in the doctor's face on the simplest of examinations. To be fair, there is a 'sensation of giving way' that can occur with a deficiency in proprioception[4], that is thought to accompany the problem of 'hypermobility' – slack ligaments in the joints. This itself is fairly easy to pick up on examination, so I'd still recommend you avoid using the phrase unless you can back it up by putting both feet behind the back of your head.

4 'Pains all over my body . . .'

There are some diseases that *can* cause pains all over the body, but in the main *proper* diseases such as *proper* arthritis will cause pains in specific areas. Indeed pains are usually in specific areas even in those diseases that *can* cause pain all over the body.[5]

---

[4] The ability of nerve-endings to tell your brains the position of all the bits of your body in space. We don't realise it exists until it's pointed out, but how else could you eat in the dark?

[5] One of which, fibromyalgia, has recently transformed from an unacceptable diagnosis 'my pains are much worse than fibromyalgia' to one enthusiastically sought 'what do you mean you don't think it's fibromyalgia?' The recent accept-ance of fibromyalgia as 'real disease' in applications such as Disability Living Allowance is almost certainly unconnected.

5 '. . . and it makes me drop things . . .'

Don't use this to impress with your 'arthritis'. Again, there are some diseases which make you drop things, but they're mainly neurological, and they're not arthritis. Since GPs are terrified by anything vaguely neurological, you'll be stuck with an eight-month wait for a neuro-appointment and nobody will look at your painful joints. Of course, if you don't have any joint pains in the first place, that'll be OK since you can complain about the length of wait.

6 'Today's a good day.'

OK. The doctor's is a bit like the dentist's, so this can be an innocent truth. But if you're saying that your joints have been swollen every single day for the past eight months, except today . . .

7 'My whole hand swells up.'

No it doesn't.

Not if it's arthritis.

But do tell me if your hand does all swell up as I'll be able to fob you off on dermatologists or somebody who looks after allergies and stuff.

8 So what's causing all these pains, then?

Most of the previous tend to occur near the beginning of the consultation, giving the doctor an early 'heads up' that all is not what it appears. This one is a late own-goal, sometimes when the doc has no previous suspicions. 'So what's causing all this pain then' is the plaintive cry after the doctor has done all his story-taking, body-examining, head-scratching (that's his own), and indeed investigation-results-perusing before coming up with the news that it's 'not rheumatoid arthritis' or 'not a heart-attack' or 'not cancer'.

And it's a dead giveaway.

Again, you may regard this as an over-interpretation. Surely the patient must still wonder what the problem is? An unexplained pain is still a big worry. But the clincher is the speed with which the question springs to the patient's mind. There is no *relief* that it's not rheumatoid arthritis, or a heart attack, or cancer. Let's face it, this is basically GOOD NEWS – but there is no sense of that. Just an immediate assertion of failure on the doctor's part to come up with an answer. And this suggests the patient was never really worried about RA/Heart attack/cancer in the first place. And if their symptoms were such that the doctor felt he was obliged to investigate for one of these diseases . . . *why* weren't *they* worried?

9 'To let you understand, doctor . . .'

Patients use this as a preamble to giving their past history of chronic illness with recurring problems. 'To let you understand, doctor, I've been having these strokes now for years . . .' They talk about a past diagnosis to lead the doctor in that direction because they have no confidence that telling him a supposedly current history would take him towards that diagnosis . . . or indeed any diagnosis. This does not mean that a patient's past history is always useless. Far from it – we always ask about past history. But first we ask about what you're feeling wrong just now. When someone who's been brought into hospital as an *emergency* starts telling you how his problem dates back twenty years rather than answering an enquiry as to what he's feeling wrong by telling you what he's feeling wrong, I struggle to be impressed.

10 'None of the tablets help at all'
Doesn't say that the patient is making it up, but can help exclude the more serious causes of the symptom. Again most obvious with joint pains. The worst of rheumatoid arthritis joints will be helped by anti-inflammatories, but the aches-and-pains of pain syndromes usually aren't. Anti-inflammatories do exactly what they say on the tin; if they don't help your pain, chances are there is NO inflammation.

A more striking example is paracetamol which often makes very little difference to a tension headache, but will relieve the headache of a brain tumour in its early days. I repeat that this doesn't mean people 'make up' tension headaches. Indeed I use them as an example to patients who refuse to believe that stress or depression or simply misfortune can cause actual pains. They will readily accept headaches as occurring without any sinister underlying disease, and the example can help them to realise that pains elsewhere can be the same.

11 'All the drugs give me side-effects'

OK.

Some people may be more prone to side-effects than others (though an over-awareness of what *might* happen usually contributes), but in general having a side-effect to one drug doesn't make you more likely to have problems with the next one. So when doctors see a patient who immediately has a new side-effect every time he/she starts a new drug, the first thought is that the patient doesn't want to take any drugs. Which makes immediate sense, since drugs are dangerous. Which makes even more sense if you don't need them. If you don't have a disease that needs drugs, don't take any.

You might be happy to have everybody believe you've got arthritis – since it stops the wife nagging you to convert the attic – but not so keen to let the doctor give you dangerous chemicals to cure the non-existent disease. So you develop side-effects as soon as you start anything, and immediately have to stop it.

Doctors will soon spot this, particularly if you blunder innocently (?) into one of the three main categories. The first includes patients that develop bizarre side-effects that no-one has ever encountered before with each of the drugs ('it makes my right elbow turn green – or is it my left?').

Conversely, the second group develop the classical characteristic side-effect for each drug – having clearly looked this up in those nice little rice-paper sheets you get crammed in beside your tablets. The third bunch get *the same symptom with every drug they try* – so head-aches are caused by the penicillin, by the gold injections, by the steroids, and by the paracetamol given for the headaches.

The last technique does have the advantage of being easy to remember under interrogation, but I believe the best plan is to mix and match the above options. That keeps some semblance of the side-effects being possibly genuine.

Hold on a minute. What am I doing?

You may be surprised that I am willing to give you advice in this area. I thought I wanted to keep your doctor happy? Well, whilst always having side-effects is a tell-tale that there's nothing wrong with you, this blunder will not upset your doctor. He has known all along that you were probably 'at it' but hasn't been convinced enough (paradoxically, didn't have 'the bottle') to NOT give you drugs. When you insist on not taking them, he's relieved as he's no longer treating you for a disease he doesn't think you have. So everybody's happy. The doctor avoids confrontation, can 'humour' you about your disease while being off the hook as far as making it better because his hands are tied, and needn't worry about poisoning you.

And you don't have to convert the attic.

★   ★   ★

Of course, you must realise that if you DO have any of the symptoms that automatically mean that you are making the whole thing up, don't let all of the above put you off. You should still tell your doctor immediately. Cos they don't *always* mean you're making it up – and doctors realise that. Not all doctors are as cynical and evil as I am. In fact, maybe none.

SYMPTOMS NOT WORTH MENTIONING AS EVERYBODY GETS THEM

1 Thinning of the hair

D octors should never ask a woman over the age of 32 if her hair is falling out. They are all convinced their hair is 'thinning' pathologically. Here's why.

You have approximately 100–150,000 hair follicles on your head. Each one goes through phases of producing a longer and longer hair for a few years, then resting, letting it fall out and starting again. This is why even if you never ever cut you hair, you still can't get it to trail behind you on the ground, much as we'd all like to. The whole cycle lasts around three/four years. And all the follicles are slightly out of sync with each other (Duh! . . . otherwise we'd all be bald for two months every three years). So if there's approximately 1,000 days in the cycle, then we must all lose approximately 100–150 of our 100–150,000 hairs *every day*. So when you go into the shower and wash your hair and a big bunch of them come away on the hair-brush, DON'T PANIC! (Patches of baldness, on the other hand, mean something.)

This sequence also explains the major thinning of hair that many women experience in the few months after their baby is born. During the pregnancy itself, the normal cycle is disturbed and the hairs whose turn it is to fall out refuse to do so (Hormones! Pah!). After the baby is born, up to nine-months' worth of hairs all fall out at the same time to 'catch up'. As if new mothers didn't have enough to worry about.

2 Fatigue

OK, it can mean something (including very important things), so you can mention it once then forget it. Don't harp on about it 'cos there's no more to tell. Particularly if it's being going on for years. Doctors all think *they're* fatigued so there's no point in trying to evoke their sympathy with long stories of fifteen different things that'll make you tired (No. 6: sitting in a chair all day listening to people telling you what makes them tired.)

3 Pain under the left breast

Sharp. Lasting less than a minute. Not associated with exercise. Not everybody gets this, but around 10% do. I get it. We've no idea what causes it, and unfortunately our name for it – '*atypical left submammary chest pain*' – does little to convince the patient that we're not side-stepping the issue, describing the problem in high-falutin' words and calling that a diagnosis. Dermatologists actually make a career out of this, but it works for them because they do it in Latin. So when a dermatologist looks all thoughtful for a while before telling you it's 'Lichen Planus', he's just using Latin words to say it's flat and thick (the area of skin, that is) or if he comes up with 'erythema multiforme' that's just a red rash with lots of different funny little shapes. Genius really. Oh yeah, then he gives you some steroid cream because that makes every rash on the planet go away. The tricky ones come back.

4 Headaches you've had all day every day for the past 14 years

Too long duration to have a sinister cause, this has to be a variation of the headache we all get. You're just not accustomed to this life-thing yet.

5 Forgetting stuff

You'd be amazed the number of people who think that forgetting where they left the house keys, or their wallet, warrants urgent investigation. We all do that. OK, it can be the earliest signs of dementia (more worrying if you forget where you left your actual house) but since we can't do much about that anyway, why worry? You won't shortly . . .

Particularly bizarre is the worry that 'I keep forgetting to do things' like telephone the bank, pay a bill (. . . erm . . .) etc. We've all got so many things to do, of course we forget some of them. There's a brilliant quote that sums up the futility of this, which I can't quite remember off the top of my head, but will append in a footnote.[1]

6 Severe lancinating pain through the eyeball lasting 2–3 seconds only

OK. *I* get this. Other doctors say they've never heard of it, but putting it in this list makes it somehow official and makes me feel less uneasy about it.

7 Patches of numbness (qv)

Pins-and-needles coming and going at no particular places of the body at no particular time but maybe when you might just possibly have been leaning against something for a while. Pah!

8 Stiffness of less than 5 minutes duration first thing in the morning . . .

. . . *oh yes . . . .and it also happens when I get up from a chair* . . . and this story coming from an 85-year-old who has to leave his clinic appointment early to get to the golf course.

9 Fingers and toes feeling cold in the cold weather

Duh!

10 Crushing chest pain with breathlessness, nausea and a cold sweat

Sorry. Wrong list.

1

TEN DON'TS AND DOS FOR MEDICAL IN-PATIENTS

1 Don't smoke

It has always been a bit demoralising on a ward round trying to figure out how to treat some guy's bronchitis while you wait for him to come back from a quick fag in the day-room. Nowadays, of course, smoking is 'banned' in hospitals. Awaiting the return from the equivalent 'fly puff' in the toilet is still not appreciated, whilst there are mixed medical views on the clutch of spluttering patients who smoulder around the front entrance. Some are aghast at the irony of having to clamber through a fug of smoke no longer tolerated in pub doorways to get into a hospital. Others feel that this downside is entirely recouped in the anti-smoking propaganda value of the public seeing an amputee coughing up his filter-tip.

2 Don't let your family and friends keep 'phoning to speak to or make an appointment with your consultant

For some reason, relatives seem to believe it's a doctor's job to keep them informed about everything that's happening to their loved one. It isn't. If anybody's, it's the patient's. The doctor tells the patient what's going on, then he/she passes on to family and friends as much of that information as he/she sees fit. When you consider the principles of doctor-patient confidentiality, the doctor shouldn't be talking to your relatives at all, certainly not until he's first checked with you.

Of course, occasionally a patient may be confused, or have trouble following or remembering things, and a chat with relatives might be to everyone's benefit. But the idea that doctors should give you a ten-minute daily update on your brother's progress is clearly nonsense. I might have 20–30 patients 'under my care' (if I'm not careful with the rota). Even at ten minutes per call (and allowing only one relative per patient!) that's more than five hours per day – leaving me no time to . . . well . . . to go and see how your brother's doing, for a start.

The idea that we can all set by a spare half-hour for a giant get together with your family is even more optimistic. These meetings can be a huge waste of everybody's time. Relatives have to come all the way up to the hospital at a specific hour (which hopefully the doctor will have ensured isn't *that* amenable). The doctor needs to make that time available – cancelling whatever he'd normally be doing – plus make sure of some breathing space before so he won't overrun and be late for the gathering. (He will not leave breathing space afterwards. Indeed, if he has any sense, the reasonable time set aside will perforce be ended by an important scheduled meeting which he is obliged to attend.) He must also read up on your recent results and treatments since relatives think that doctors know at all times everything that's happening to all their patients. (To illustrate which, witness a genuine phone call switched without warning through to my office some years back:

'Hello? . . . Hello?'

'Hello Doctor, what was the result of my mother's scan?')

Once the meeting is underway, each relative will require to have their say as they vie to show how much they care about you. They have to justify their presence, and indeed the meeting itself. So even if the doctor's initial blurb explains absolutely everything they could possibly want to know, they'll still have to ask lots of questions. Except in exceptional circumstances, these meetings should be avoided like the plague (incidentally, very much not one of the exceptional circumstances).

★　★　★

Do, when the doctor asks if it's OK for him to talk about your case to your relatives . . . *refuse permission*. The doc will love you for it.

3 Don't threaten to sign yourself out

Whether you think the doctors are being overcautious and there's nothing wrong with you (including when you were pretending in the first place), or you have three cats back home that need their Kennomeat, or you're supposed to be getting a plane to Lanzarote . . . don't threaten to 'self-discharge against medical advice'.

It gives everybody so much hassle.

The nurses will have to inform their bosses. Then the junior doctor on-call that's never seen you before will be called to persuade you against your proposed action. Meantime at least one nurse will be detailed to keep an eye on you, preventing her from having that hour's tea-break. By the time the pissed-off junior arrives, you'll have changed your mind and want to stay. But to do this immediately would lose face, as well as marking you down as a 'waster', so you'll be obliged to keep up a convincing front of wanting to go home immediately, while the doctor's obliged to keep up a convincing front of wanting you to stay in. So everybody has to waste 30–60 minutes of their life in a Mexican stand-off with the added twist that each would be happiest with the outcome that the other is arguing for . . .

★　　★　　★

Do actually sign yourself out. Promptly. No fuss. As long as you're absolutely *sure* there's nothing wrong with you.

4 **Don't wander around the ward from day one, in some self-help-psychology attempt to convince yourself that you're perfectly fit and healthy**

a) The consultant on his ward-round will get miffed while he's waiting for people to find you.

b) He'll take your manoeuvre at face value and wonder what you're doing in his emergency ward in the first place.

c) The nurses and consultant will fall out over why a man with a suspected heart-attack and potential for sudden cardiac arrest is down in the canteen buying muffins.

Do sit nicely in your bed in your pyjamas until the ward-round reaches you and you are seen and examined.

. . . *then* go for a smoke . . .

5 **Don't play a radio**

– particularly if the ward-round is on (no, not on the radio . . .), and particularly particularly if they're about to see you. Any self-respecting consultant's request for you to switch it off will inevitably cause some unnecessary frostiness between you, whilst the non-self-respecting consultant will wear out his stethoscope's diaphragm trying to differentiate the machinery-murmur of pericarditis from Smashing Pumpkins.

6 Don't pretend to be asleep

Not sure why they do it. But the occasional patient on a post-receiving ward round doesn't seem to notice my arrival at their bed. On gently prodding them, they wake up all confused and blinded by the light and stuff. Which immediately makes me think . . . if *I* was waiting for the Bigbossman (lol) to come round and find out what's wrong with me, I'd be on the edge of my wits with anticipation . . . unless I knew the answer was 'nothing much[1]'.

7 Don't ask your consultant a question when he's standing at the ward trolley dealing with another case

This might seem different from stopping him in the corridor, but it isn't. Even when he can see what bed you're in, is standing beside all the case-notes, *even if you're the patient he's just finished dealing with*, he won't remember anything about your case. This isn't because he doesn't care, or is dementing (necessarily). It's to do with focus. All the world's best bridge players will tell you

---

[1] OK. Occasionally somebody does genuinely fall asleep. You can tell by the way they wake up.

that part of their secret is to concentrate on the current hand; no distractions, no giving themselves a mental hug about what they did or didn't do on the previous deal. So if you ask me something at the case trolley, I'll have no idea who you are. And it's because I'm *too* focussed. That's also why I can't remember what I had for breakfast . . .

8 Don't carry on loud conversations with other patients during the ward round

It's tricky enough taking a history, examining a patient and . . . thinking, without a bunch of guys battering on about last night's match on the other side of the screens. Last month I was unconvinced about my diagnosis of pericarditis for an emergency admission as I couldn't hear any 'friction rub' – a crunching sound the two linings of the heart make against each other when they're inflamed – with my stethoscope. The next day, the murmur was blatant. I wondered if the signs had changed or if I was getting even more deaf before realising – the patient was now in a side-room.

So if you do engage in a five-way conversation which the others continue whenever it's your own turn to be examined – just don't complain when the doc doesn't spot that your heart's about to explode.

9 Do laugh at the consultant's jokes

unless they are aimed at the nurses. Your quality-of-life in the ward depends much more on being in *their* good books.

10 Don't let your relatives keep phoning up the nurses to ask how you are doing

They've actually got work to do. My theory is that we should earmark one relative at the time of admission who is allowed to phone up for information. Then every other relative or friend can get their info from him or her. Amongst other advantages, this would avoid this genuine conversation I overheard (well, half of) in my own ward.

R: *How is my brother doing?*
N: *He had quite a settled night.*
R: *What? My other brother phoned up just five minutes ago and you told him that he hadn't slept that well!!*

To which the nurse, to her credit, did not reply SO WHY DID YOU ASK???

11 Don't wear powerful perfume

It spoils the bouquet of the wine with dinner.

PRIVATE MEDICINE

Private medicine isn't a bad thing.
  Hmmm. I don't disagree with that (after all, I wrote it), but my innate left-of-centredness isn't entirely happy . . . we'll start again . . .

Private medicine is not necessarily a bad thing.

In most transactions in life, somebody gives us something, or renders us a service – and we pay them. The plumber comes round, fixes the tap – and we pay him. We take the car to the garage, the mechanic fixes it – and we pay him. The Estate Agent sells our house (well, actually, puts a blurry photo of it in the paper while we sell it) – and we pay him (plus 'extra' for the blurry photo). In most countries, going to see a doctor is pretty much the same thing. But here in the UK, we have the NHS – which is, if you think about it, one of the most totally brilliant ideas ever. Whenever you get sick, somebody, indeed lots of people, look after you and you don't pay them. You get looked after for free. It's the way it should be, and it's great.

But.

Because anybody can get healthcare free, it doesn't follow that it's wrong for someone to pay for healthcare. That doesn't really make sense – unless their paying for healthcare is in some way stopping someone else from getting it, and there's no real evidence for that. Even if we baulk at the possibility that somebody paying-for-it might get better or faster healthcare, that's more a mental-set than a thought-through moral stance. It still doesn't make it wrong – unless this interferes with *your* healthcare. Again, no evidence that it does. Perhaps even the opposite is the case. If you're tenth in line waiting to get your hip replaced, and two of the guys in front of you go pay to get it done privately – you're now eighth in line and will get it done earlier. We could go back to the Estate Agent (though that phrase pains me) analogy. It would be really good if we used public money to ensure everyone in the country had a decent house to live in. Everyone. For free. But that wouldn't suddenly mean it was wrong for someone to buy a bigger house. And to give up on the whole scheme because more and more people were buying big houses would be crazy.

However.

What if the guy who should be doing your hip is the same guy who is away doing the two guys ahead of you in the queue *and* doing two other guys who should be behind you? This is the principal worry of most people concerned about 'queue-jumping'. NHS consultants 'moonlighting'.

The glib answer is that he almost certainly isn't doing the private hips whilst otherwise he could be in an NHS hospital going through that waiting-list. The facilities are likely not available. The NHS has its financial and logistic limitations. If it could (or . . . wanted to?), it might build another operating-theatre and pay this guy, plus extra anaesthetists and nursing staff, to do more NHS hips – but at the moment it isn't. So chances are the operating theatres are fully-booked doing other things, and whether the surgeon goes and does private cases in his spare time doesn't really matter.

Theoretically.

The answer is glib as it ignores the potential for the abuse of this situation. Consultants could 'create' spare time in their working week to do loads of private cases. The recent change in the consultants' contract was supposedly an attempt to close this loophole – making them work more rigid schedules – but in reality that's government propaganda that doctors themselves are happy to let you believe. The real reason for the new contract was that consultants *wanted more money* – particularly for the overtime hours for which they received no payment at all. When it reached the stage they were considering industrial action (though clearly had no idea what that might entail[1]), the Government, not wishing to appear

---

[1] Since writing, doctors have actually 'gone on strike' and had no idea what to do.

to be backing down, came up with the face-saving idea of saying a new contract was *their* idea. They would pay doctors precisely for the hours they worked, increasing control and return for their money. Unfortunately their negotiators who calculated these payments assumed the government's other main piece of propaganda – that doctors spent all their time on the golf course – was true. When it turned out most doctors worked 8–10 hours more per week than they'd previously been paid for, the bill to the taxpayer was huge. And they still had no new abilities to spot the chancers who *do* spend all their time on the golf course.

So six years down the line, the 'face-saving' propaganda backfires and the entire country is complaining because all this money has been pumped into the NHS and there's nothing to show for it. There never was going to be – any more than agreeing to a wage demand from teachers could lead to more children being taught. Of course, consultants also look a bit shady in the light of such a good deal. But they were on this occasion less upset than usual at being painted as the baddies, as now at least they were quite well-paid baddies.

We seem to have gone off at a tangent. All right, *I* seem to have. I'm supposed to be giving you tips on dealing with private medicine, not justifying its relationship with NHS politics. But you'll be wondering how keeping your 'private' doctor happy can be any different from keeping your NHS doctor happy – particularly since it's the same guy wearing a better jacket and tie. Well, it can. A change in his priorities induces a change in yours, and the following manoeuvres suddenly become *de rigueur*.

1 Turn up for your appointment – or let him know well in advance if you can't

In the NHS, we like to pretend that it upsets us when a patient doesn't turn up to the clinic. In reality, we're pleased. If lots fail to appear, we're over the moon. First off, it's simply less work to do that afternoon. Secondly, when we are made aware of the absentees at the clinic's early finish, we can sift through the case-sheets of the 'non-attenders' or 'DNAs' (a nicely scientific phrase for Did-Not-Attends), deciding whether to send them a further appointment or discharge them from the clinic. Thus we can get shot of a large tranche of patients who are tricky, annoying, or have a form of nothing-wrong-with-them that, either through fear or uncertainty, we've found ourselves unable to point out to them over the years. The first time any of these characters' buses fails to turn up, they're out on their ear.

But Private Clinics are different. They have more precise booking systems – each patient in his amply-allotted time-slot. Let's say I'm a consultant doing a private clinic. A patient's failure to turn up is immediately discernible since I'm stuck in my little consulting-room, twiddling my thumbs for forty minutes until my 'three o'clock' arrives. It's a much clearer waste of my time, since I could have slotted another (paying) patient into the vacancy. Not only that, but – and here my standard comparisons with plumber and garage mechanic give way to a much more revealing analogy with an even older profession – *I have already paid for the room.*

All other things being equal, I should send you a bill.

2 Turn up for your appointment – on time

As mentioned above, Private Clinics have more precise timings than the NHS. The latter works on the basic principle of always-having-some-patients-around for the doctor to see. So none of his time is wasted. They are therefore 'front-loaded' with a disproportionate number of appointments near the start. This makes some sense, since if there were lots of appointments near the end, and some early-appointment people turned up late, or were particularly tricky, the last stages of the clinic would be chaos. (In the old days, avoidance of this was at the extreme level of giving all patients the same appointment time at the start of the clinic. Even I find that cruel.) Because of this, no-show patients at the start don't result in forty minutes of thumb-twiddling. But it does mean that patients often have to wait longer than they really should as the doctors wade through the deliberately manufactured backlog if everybody turns up.

Private patients would clearly 'not tolerate' such treatment, so each has a specific time slot allocated to them. More generous than normal, and the doctor has some chance to keep to it. But it's fairly inflexible, particularly since there are no accompanying 'juniors' to paper over any cracks. So, in the NHS, you're forty minutes late and you simply join the queue a bit later. In private practice, if you have a starting appointment for 2pm and you don't turn up until 2.40, the doctor will have done his thumb-twiddling and now started on his second patient. When he finishes, he will go onto his third, rather than have them wait while he sees you. They have, after all, an appointment and have turned up in time for it. And so on. Unless someone else fails to turn up, you will have to wait to the end of the session to see him. At which point, if he's fully booked, his renting of the room will be over and another doctor may be coming in, leaving the pair of you scouting round for a spare couch.

So turn up on time.

3 Know the details of your insurance cover
Not the Policy Number, or the validation number, or the helpline number (we're really not in a rush for these, though the hospital might be) – just know what you have actually got covered. It's bad news all round if you and your doctor both assume that you're 'insured' and he does a big bunch of blood tests and Xrays (£70 a zap) and the odd scan or two (£300–£1000 a za-a-ap) before your Insurance company points out that you've got the 'Special Premium Silver Star' policy which covers

167

you for one doctor's appointment and thirteen-pounds-fifty worth of investigations.[2]

Such 'misunderstandings' may arise from the usual unhelpful vagueness of financial institutions, but here my medical-vs-surgical paranoia also raises its head. Most insurance 'deals' are geared towards surgery, and will often cover a single outpatient appointment with basic tests, making more cash available only when you come in for your operation. The idea that there might not be an operation – that the doctor might diagnose your problem, give you some helpful tablets, and follow you up – no more occurs to them than to Stephen Spielberg when script-writing an episode for ER. For us medical chaps who spend our time trying to work out what's wrong from history and examination (rather than slicing into a likely area and seeing what colour everything looks) then getting your GP to prescribe the correct sort of tablets (rather than chopping out anything vaguely green) and ensuring these *were* correct, this insurance approach doesn't work too well. The patient thus ends up with a huge bill including investigation fees as well as consultant fees The consultant feels he has to reduce his fees to try to alleviate the burden and everybody is left unhappy. Except the insurance company . . . and, of course, the surgeons.

---

[2] The immediate doctor-reaction – to reduce his own fee – often backfires as the company *has* covered this part of the transaction and we end up just saving *them* more money.

4 Don't Go Private to 'skip the queue' unless you intend to manage the whole disease episode privately

This tip's mainly for uninsured patients, and mainly for surgical problems. If there's a six-month NHS wait to be seen about your hernia, you can indeed see a surgeon in a private clinic within a week or two for, say £100. But if he diagnoses the hernia and plans the op, that'll cost hundreds, maybe thousands. 'Skipping the queue' by paying this, we all agreed earlier (?!), is OK. But you can't at this stage decide 'that's too much' and get the operation done free on the NHS, having paid a relatively minor £100 to skip past everyone else. The consultant can't now put you onto his NHS operating list. Not even at the end of it, since that would still skip the weeks you would normally wait simply for the clinic appointment.

The ethics of this become trickier if it's a more serious, or life-threatening problem. Hernia, bunion, maybe even joint replacement can be done whenever it can be arranged. There's no rush, though the patient will suffer unnecessary discomfort in the meantime. But if the doctor discovers a cancer[3], and you can't afford the operation?

Actually, taking it to this extreme suddenly makes

[3] I use the common example against my better judgement. Cancer is NOT always the most urgent of situations. But no time here to challenge years of media brain-washing.

169

it easy. The consultant can transfer you promptly to the NHS via your GP as, with the information your GP now has, any NHS facility would be seeing you very quickly anyway.

As always, it's the middling cases that are the trickiest. A patient with bowel symptoms doesn't want to wait the four months to even see an NHS gastroenterologist so goes private. He agrees she needs an expensive investigation (e.g. a colonoscopy, with an NHS wait of 2–3 months) to exclude a cancer which she may or may not have. The patient baulks at the price. Can she go straight onto the NHS lists for the test – or does she have to wait even to get a clinic appointment? If she does go onto the colonoscopy list, can she go ahead of anybody else? Certainly not because of her 'private' status (unthinkable), but what if the consultant thinks her story is really very suspicious of cancer, and you'd want to find out quickly. Say there is a routine list (maybe accessible directly by GPs) for people unlikely to have serious disease, but another fast one for those with scarey symptoms? Which one does she go on? Her case is urgent, but others on the routine list may not have had the benefit of an expert opinion which could similarly tell that their story was not 'routine'.

If the NHS could do all the things we'd like it to – instant appointments . . . instant investigations . . . instant treatments – the above wouldn't arise. But it can't (though recent reductions in waiting-times have improved things). And there's no easy answer.

But it has to be said, that's the doctor's problem. Not yours. So this tip is really to help avoid the doctor having a dilemma, rather than a tip to help *you*. Might as well tell you 'be rich.'

5 Don't Call the Consultant at Home

Some patients paying to see a doctor privately seem to think this gives them access to him at all times. Whilst some private physicians tolerate or even encourage this (usually because they are keen to build up a huge private practice and give up NHS medicine altogether), I for one refused to do so for three good reasons.

Firstly, the patient should realise that their money gets them to see the doctor at set times. They should not confuse 'private physician' with 'personal physician'. The latter suggests I be permanently on-call for any problems which crop up, and would involve my being constantly paid for said being-on-call – like a personal physician to the President, or the Aga Khan, or Blofeld. And that would be instead of my other job – you know, the one at the hospital. You don't phone your private accountant at 9pm because you've come home to a bill from the taxman. If it is a genuine medical emergency, that may be different (though personally, I'd go to an NHS emergency department because they're much better at that sort of thing . . . and you won't need to phone your private accountant-person), but fortunately rarely a worry for a rheumatologist.

Secondly, I'm quite a lazy person.

Thirdly, I might be drunk.

6 Pay Your Bill

Seems self-evident. But many people appear to think doctors are above that sort of thing (money), or perhaps that they'll be too embarrassed to chase you for it – and to some extent that's true. My limited experience of private medicine quickly made me aware of the major hassles entailed in working outside the NHS. No back-up from juniors (most people regard the main advantage of being seen privately as always seeing the consultant – but any doctor with insight knows the opposite is true since occasionally being seen by the side-kick helps make sure Bossperson isn't missing anything), no help keeping clinical records, no help keeping financial records, having to deal with the Inland Revenue – including such esoterics as deciding whether 'an interim advance payment as a balance of previous debits' means that I owe the tax-man money or he owes me . . .

But the worst thing is trying to chase up unpaid bills. Firstly, it just doesn't feel right to demand money from an ill person. Admittedly those who don't pay are more likely to have absolutely nothing wrong with them; a double-think psyche having decided to take umbrage at the consultant spotting this and retaliating by not paying his fees. Arguably, the nothing-wrong-with-them patient is slightly less common in the private sector. When they do turn up, they raise an extra ethical dilemma. Often the easiest approach for the consultant would be to pretend you're even worse at your job than in reality and act like you do believe the patient has some trumped-up illness. While one often does this in the NHS just to keep the peace, it does feel more morally dubious when that also keeps the money rolling in.

The other major non-paying psyche has never had any intention of paying the bill in the first place, hoping the doctor will find it too awkward to hire a lawyer, or send the boys round (particularly since the doctor might suspect the patient would have access to bigger boys).

Since we are not only poorly motivated to chase cash, but also unskilled at record-keeping and the use of the baseball bat, paying your bill with any sort of normal promptness is hugely appreciated.

One more thing. As far as the doctor is concerned, you come to see him, he sees you, and you pay him. You may or may not have some deal with an insurance company to cover your debts – but that's not really his concern, so don't expect *him* to go chasing *them*.

ALTERNATIVE MEDICINE

U nless you're Prince Charles (in which case you'll probably get away with it[1]) I'd advise against mentioning alternative (complementary) medicine to the doctor. It's not that we're all totally against the idea. Many doctors have a reasonably open mind, and some are ardent enthusiasts (though such a touchy-feely stance makes the rest of us question their conventional-doctor-acumen. We Darth Vader types are always suspicious of those who turn to the 'Bright Side'). The problem is that the mere mention of alternative medicine can alter the focus of a consultation. At worst, the doctor will indeed be a conventional anti-Alternative and will henceforth view you as some sort of nutcase whose now unhidden agenda means he can't trust a thing you tell him. Even the

[1] And if you are Prince Charles, thanks for buying the book, Your Royal Highness. And how about a Royal commendation, or a retrospective foreword? You don't need to say it's the best, funniest book in the whole world; just that people should keep an open mind, and give it a chance . . .

174

more enlightened practitioner will be slightly uncomfortable with everything he's doing and suggesting, in case it sparks some reaction *vis-a-vis* its presumptuousness (like meeting someone at a party that you are forewarned is a raging feminist and you have to rethink your approach to 90% of your conversation topics . . . well, I have).

But wait. It's generally assumed that people should let their doctor know everything about their case, and surveys say more than 40% of patients attending hospital are also taking alternative remedies – so how can I tell you not to mention alternative medicines? OK, then. Just don't mention it too early in the conversation. Wait until the doctor has done most of his history-taking and examination and planning and then gently wonder aloud how complementary medicine might fit into this. Then we can have a sensible discussion after the doctor has had a chance to put his plan together in normal fashion.

If this is all to go smoothly, it's going to need some give-and-take on both sides. The doc who thinks alternative medicine is codswallop shouldn't belittle patients for thinking it's the bees' knees[2]. That's a given. The doctor must make some effort to 'keep an open mind'. Incidentally, this assertion has always been the master-stroke for alternativists against the conventionalists. As long as you keep

[2] A trusty cure for rheumatism when made into a rejuvenating tea.

175

claiming that all you ask is for everyone to keep 'an open mind' (i.e. that the other side admit your remedies *might* work), how can anyone disagree? You are being so eminently reasonable. The medical establishment opposition are now in a cleft stick. Either they insist you're wrong (and *they* now look like unreasonable extremists) or they have to say out loud that your stuff might work. And that admission is all you need to sell your remedies-with-no-side-effects to the world. Genius!

On the other hand, the patient shouldn't treat the doctor with hostility just because he *doesn't* believe in these things. He is paid to know about conventional medical matters and have a considered opinion on them. If you feel strongly your doctor should believe in alternative medicine, and he doesn't – go find another doctor. If you're a Catholic who's wanting some 'religious' guidance and you've gone to the synagogue by accident, you don't try to convert the rabbi to Catholicism so that he can give you the advice you wanted in the first place – you go see a priest.[3]

So if we're going to be all sensible about it, the first thing we have to acknowledge is that Alternative Medicine isn't just one thing, and realise that each of the different modalities might independently be good, bad or indifferent. Anyone who suggests

---

[3] Or Garage Analogy No. 23: 'I insist that *you* fix my car, but instead of using engine oil you must use woodland primrose juice.'

that all Alternative Medicine must be good because . . . well . . . it's alternative, is clearly not worth the discussion. Alternative comedy isn't *all* funny just because it's alternative. So if I put down here the doctor's view (as I see it – so it's clearly one of those well-balanced ones) of some of the alternative approaches, you'll see where we're coming from and that might lead to more fruitful discussions (I'll drop the United Nations posture shortly).

Homoeopathy

Lots of people believe they can trust homoeopathy because it's 'natural' and has been around for thousands of years. Except, it isn't and it hasn't. It was 'invented' by a renegade doctor called William Hannemann in the early nineteenth century. Having fallen foul of the medical Establishment (no disgrace in that – I hope), he decided to devise his own approach. From the simple observation that quinine both causes fever and treats malaria (famously associated with a fever), he decided that 'like treats like' – or *similia similibus curantur*, as we passive Latin scholars like to put it. If a drug or substance causes a symptom, then that drug can be used to treat a person who has that symptom. (bit of a jump, but that's how you make a name for yourself). Presumably realising that, for example, pumping strychnine into a young child who started off with vomiting just

177

might be counterproductive, he decided that we should use ridiculously small amounts of the drug. Literally 'vanishingly small' amounts since a quantity of the substance is diluted, say 1:10, in water and shaken (not stirred – known as *succussion*). Then a small portion of the resultant 'mixture' is diluted a further ten times . . . then again . . . then again . . . then . . . The number of times this is done can often be seen on the bottle (6x, 10x, 30x).

Interestingly, the 30x preparations prompted some scientifically-minded, mathematically-entranced, mean-spirited doctor-types (there are three of us) to point out that after 30 such dilutions there are absolutely NO molecules of the original substance left in the liquid[4]. None. Homoeopathists were (reasonably) quick to explain that the water molecules themselves were changed by all that succussion stuff and could 'remember' the substance that had been diluted away – but it was always going to be difficult to persuade us cynical guys that this was anything other than an afterthought (syn. 'tosh').

[4] All to do with a thing called *Avogadro's Number* which is the number of molecules of a substance in its own 'atomic weight' in grams. It's stupidly high (e.g. 602,214,150,000,000,000,000,000 atoms in 12 grams of carbon) but not *infinitely* high. So if you keep diluting something, there will eventually be none left – essentially you're taking one 'zero' off every time you dilute one-in-ten.

Practitioners of Homoeopathy focus on each and every one of your symptoms, rather than pursuing an over-all diagnosis to explain them as a whole. They then prescribe a number of their preparations which will deal with all of these. They have usually trained first as physicians, though are largely happiest if you separately attend a conventional doctor.

The conventional doctor himself will meantime be quite happy if you express a wish to try homoeopathy – just don't ask him to say that he thinks it works. (The most famous *homoeopathist* of my acquaintance would always refuse to say aloud that *he* thinks it works.) And don't expect them to refer you to someone. Your financial adviser may well be open-minded as to whether Gypsy Rose Lee really can foretell the future ('one day you will give this all up and become a stripper . . .'), but is unlikely to send you to her for stock market tips.

So keep your conventional doctor happy by letting him know about your homoeopathy, but not insisting he believes in it. Keep your homoeopathist happy by . . . doing the same thing (and not stopping any conventional medicines unless he tells you, or without telling your doctor).

Herbal Medicine

It's undeniable that herbal medicines have a chance of working. Many conventional drugs are old herbal remedies which have been purified or altered so that they can be given in precise quantities. Aspirin comes from a pain-killing and anti-fever substance in willow bark. Digoxin is an almost direct derivative from *Digitalis* (foxglove).

So many substances currently termed 'herbal remedies' will have genuine effects. Research shows that Evening Primrose Oil has effects on prostaglandins in the body and this might indeed help arthritic pains. St John's Wort also seems to have a genuine action in depression. These actions, however, are as yet not well enough established and quantified to allow their use as conventional drugs. Other herbal remedies may also be effective, and just because we can't prove this, or show an understandable way for them to work does not mean that they don't.

It's clear, therefore, that doctors should admit the possibility that a herbal remedy may have an effect. But they should differ from 'enthusiasts' in the realisation that any such remedy can also cause harm. Just because a substance occurs 'naturally' does not make it automatically 'non-toxic', as Socrates would say. None of us would eat random mushrooms we found in a pretty forest. Anything which has an effect on the body can have a side-effect, so we must realise that herbal remedies are potentially active preparations given in imprecise doses with potential for harm or interaction with other drugs. St John's Wort can decrease the blood levels of a number of conventional drugs – for instance the immunosuppressant ciclosporin, thus increasing the likelihood of transplant rejection – as well as having possible psychological side-effects of its own. So you must know about these before using it. And that's just when you know what you're getting, from a reliable source. Some years back there was a fad for people buying 'Black Balls from China' for their arthritis. Quite an enduring fad as it happened . . . because they worked. Eventually, chemical analysis explained the surprise. The Black Balls contained large doses of corticosteroids ('cortisone' . . . 'steroids'). Perhaps more worryingly they also contained three different anti-inflammatory drugs, and most impressive of all were the potentially toxic doses of heavy metals including mercury and cadmium.

Acupuncture

Works. For some things.

At least, I think it does. Not quite sure why, but sticking needles in the right places seems, for example, to reduce the pains in some joints. Suggested explanations include the release of 'endorphins' (the body's own morphine-like pain-killers) as a reaction to the needle, or a simple 'distraction' effect whereby a stimulus elsewhere takes your mind off the original pain (at a genuine level of the brain processes only being able to deal with a certain number of things at a time – 'The Gate Theory of Pain').

Research to prove any of this is rather hindered by its often being performed by 'enthusiasts' who feel obliged to be true to the ancient theories of acupuncture. Thus, after sophisticated statistical analysis of acute-phase-proteins in the blood has indeed suggested a benefit from the acupuncture, they interpret this as being due to relieving the blockage of *qi* through the body, since arthritis is basically a disease of *bi* – a blockage of the flow that normally keeps everything in balance. Makes sense at the *Yin-Yang* level, but doesn't persuade Western authorities to buy up shiploads of *zhen* for NHS clinics (that's like, *needles*, maybe it should be *zhens*).

Many NHS medics, physiotherapists and others do, however, make use of the technique. Disappointingly they often ignore the classical Acupuncture points in ancient Chinese charts, and don't follow the magical '*Gall Bladder*' and '*Spinal Warmer*' chains. More often they focus on the area of actual pain – though this itself has an equivalent in the classical *A-Shi* point – that nearest to the focus of the problem.

Chiropractic

This was invented by DD Palmer (1845–1915) who went around America showing how manipulating a person's spine could cure a variety of ills – not just joint pains. The story goes he made his name by curing a janitor's deafness in this way.

182

Most people, however, tend to associate the technique with an attempt to treat joint problems – often in the spine itself. As I've outlined in the past, anyone attending a chiropracter (or osteopath – the difference is too tricky for me to . . . er . . . explain) will be examined, then told that they have a slight misalignment of the spine (unless you have a major misalignment of the spine – I'm not sure what you're told then). This is followed by the practitioner doing that expert running-his-hands-down-your-spine thing, making them crackle like a domino-chain, after which you feel oddly invigorated. As far as I am aware, this happens no matter what your complaint. Unless you're a janitor with deafness, whereupon I assume they miss out that whole telling you about the misalignment bit and just fix it.

Copper Bangles etc.
See 'GIFTS'.

Copper Bangles etc.
OK. That was a bit unfair. Copper bangles have been used for years to improve arthritic pains. There has never really been any evidence they do anything (other than turn your wrist a bit green), but they're harmless (other than turning your wrist a bit green), and there is that thing with the magnetic torcs . . .

Shouldn't really tell you this, but you will know about these metal bangles with the magnets in the 'torc' position on the palmar side of your wrists. Supposed to help arthritis. Of course they don't.

Somebody did a study.

They compared torc-bangles with magnets against torc-bangles with no magnets and . . . the bangles with magnets did better. Of course, the wearers could tell the ones with magnets, tell that they were in the 'active treatment' group and there's the potential psychological effect. Except . . . they had two 'placebo' groups. In one, the bangles had no magnets. In the other, the bangles had magnets . . . strong enough to pick up needles etc. and 'fool' the wearer into thinking these were the active bangles – but not strong enough to actually work (according to current bangle-theory).

And the patients who had the proper strong magnets . . . did better than the ones who were fooled into *thinking* they had the proper magnets . . .

MAL'S PRACTICE

The GP Perspective

Much of the unerringly essential information and advice in this book is relevant to both hospital and General Practice settings. However, some aspects will be unique to the GP scenario (or 'surgery' as it's known). Since my experience of this is limited, I sought the help of GP-brother who (after three weeks of my waiting for an appointment) supplied me with some insights which I have written up below.

No. I refuse to call it 'Primary Care'.

Yes. His name *is* Mal.

RECEPTIONISTS

Contacting the GP surgery re appointments etc. is not the same as contacting the hospital. In the latter, the records-department-person will deal not only with a huge number of patients, but also a huge number of doctors. Many they will not know personally; some they wouldn't recognise if they bumped into them in the corridor, or the car park. Certainly the records-person will generally be indifferent to the doctor's feelings *viz-a-viz* any changes in his clinic numbers, timings, or even location.

The GP receptionist is different.

She will either adore her 'boss' with an all-subsuming, tender, unrequited (usually) love, worshipping the water he/she walks on . . . or hate his/her guts.

Find out which it is and couch all of your appointment, prescription and other requests accordingly.

PRACTICE NURSES

When I were a lad, all the best sisters on the wards eventually disappeared to become 'district nurses' (now not-at-all known as *long-term condition nurses* which is apparently interesting as they apparently refuse to do any routine manoeuvres such as blood checks pertaining to long-term conditions . . . apparently). In the modern corporate NHS, it is more likely they will be internally promoted – though again, out of the wards. Indeed they appear to follow the well-recognised 'Peter Principle' where staff are promoted within an organisation until they are one step above the level at which they are any good. Understandable when you think of it . . . be good at your job, get promoted . . . be good at your new job, get promoted . . . eventually get to a job you're clearly rubbish at, don't get promoted. Stay where you are, forever. Unfortunately the organisation ends up full of people doing jobs they're rubbish at (except for my own department's brilliant nurse-management persons . . .), and perfectly excellent Ward Sisters go round the hospital with a tick-box clip-board and a toilet-scrubber-detector because they're now in charge of the 'Infection Control' for SE Scotland and Wales.

Fortunately not all the best nurses go down the managerial route. Some stick to wards, and some indeed still go out to the districts (maybe I should say *practices*. 'District Nurse' does rather conjure up the image of trundling her bike across a mountain stream while trying to keep the flowing hemlines above water-level).

So keep your GP happy by giving your Practice Nurse her due. She knows what she's doing, and doesn't need you running off to see your GP all the time to check everything's OK. That way she gets to hold onto her autonomy, and he gets to hold onto his coffee and biscuits.

DOCTORS

GPs are simple folk. Otherwise they'd get a proper job in a hospital, or making things and stuff. At university you spot the potential GPs because you can't spot them. They're not clugging everything that moves – until it doesn't – on the rugby field (*surgeons*); nor continually swotting for exams (*physicians*); nor standing at elections for Year Club committees (*doctor-managers* e.g. the Chief Medical Officer); nor perpetually absent as they're down at the bookies (*gynaecologist to the Royal Family*). They're ordinary Joes, who just get on with things. Since they are used to flying under the radar, even in the surgery it won't always be obvious to you exactly what their position is – though it is important for you to find out.

GP Registrars (ST1s . . . ST2s . . . and various other gradings I don't understand).

When I were *still* a lad, newly-qualified doctors considering a career in general practice finished their residency year then embarked on a 'GP rotation', official or self-selected, which gave them 3–6 month spells in an eclectic mix of specialties, knowledge of which might prove useful in later years. So Accident & Emergency departments had juniors planning to be A&E consultants plus GP-types, Obstetrics and Gynaecology had embryonic O&G consultants and GP-types, Paediatrics had . . . you get the drift. They spent these months as general dogsbody to their more favoured colleague (e.g. holding the fort in the labour ward while the future Queen's Gynaecologist galloped off to Ascot) doing most of the on-call, seeing thousands of patients. One upshot was that whilst they were Jacks-of-all-trades, they actually became masters of one or two.

And if they came through one specialty and

decided, 'Hey! I'm enjoying this' or even, 'Hey! I'm really good at this' they could change tack and stick to it. Geriatricians were the classic case. Many of them came across the specialty's special appeal (you can sleep at nights) during their GP rotations.

Today the medical neonate is pretty much told on day one to decide where their career lies. They are given a label and a number and are sent round the houses not as a doctor, but as a *trainee* – because training has to be taken seriously. So instead of seeing thousands of patients, they see educational supervisors and clinical supervisors who fill out reports based on DOTS and MINICEX[1] and '360-degree-assessments' where the trainee gets their pals and nurses and nurses' pals to say how brilliant they are (all done by ticking boxes on the computer where only the most churlish colleague would tick anything other than 'excellent'). Any time they do spend on the ward is also centred on the computer requesting investigations, or looking up results of investigations, or emailing the biochemist asking why there aren't any results of investigations ('because you forgot that taking-blood-off-the-patient bit').

After two years of that, who would let them anywhere near a patient?

Well, your GP does.

[1] Doctors Online Training System . . . Mini-Clinical Evaluation EXercise . . . Yup. I don't care either.

189

He's forced to.

And the GP-surgery scenario doesn't lend itself to their normal hands-off, other people will do the real medicine, approach. The GP-registrar is forced to go heads-up with the patient at their appointed surgery and all-of-a-sudden is faced with the real world. My assumption has always been that this is why in recent years I've been inundated with referrals to the specialist rheumatology service that would embarrass any 'proper' practitioner.

Dear Rheumatologist, this lovely 85-year-old lady has had osteoarthritis (that's wear-and-tear to you . . . and me) *in her hands for 35 years. They're still a bit sore at times, particularly after a game of badminton. Could you see and advise.*[2]

Honest. Though I made up the bit about badminton – it was golf.

But another part of me was less convinced. Surely in two years they would pick up *some* knowledge? It's not that different from the old GP

---

[2] 'Please see and advise.' Classic hackle-raising phrase for hospital doctors. One GP with notoriously unhelpful letters eventually referred one chap to our local A&E saying only 'Please see and advise.' No history. No examination findings. No nothing. After dealing with the patient's problems, the Casualty officer wrote back to the GP . . . 'Seen and advised.'

rotations. Except . . . the old rotations put together a wide experience before sallying forth into GP-land. Not only do the current guys spend all their time on computers, their rota is also properly constructed between hospitals and 'primary care', properly randomised, so the trainee often *starts* in the general practice scenario.

So if your allocated GP-person looks like he's just signed the old 'S-forms' with Partick Thistle, give him a break. He's likely petrified. Yours will be the first rash he's had to diagnose on his own. And he's not being rude using his mobile phone, he's trying desperately to find pictures of a rash that look like yours. And if it's Christmas, and you do want to keep him happy – forget all that stuff I told you in 'Gifts' and get him an X-Box.

Locums

GP locums are a disparate bunch of characters. The main clue as to what-they're-doing-here comes from their age.

Young locums may simply be filling awkward spaces between jobs, 'showing willing' as they gain extra experience, or supplementing their hospital pay to finance a partner's gambling or shopping habit.

Elderly locums are likely retired GPs (or hospital practitioners) drawn back to the fold to do an old friend a favour, supplement their pension to finance their white Burgundy habit, or simply because they miss it.

It's the middle-aged ones that are tricky.

They are the ones most likely to have the background of a faltering career, financing a magic mushrooms habit, or have suffered some hiccup which may or may not involve the GMC and running off with the Children's Ward Christmas Fund, or its Staff Nurse. Of course, they are also the most likely to be the best doctor on the planet who just happens to dislike the constraints of a job-for-life and goes round the country helping as many patients as he can whilst quietly humming The Eagles' *Desperado*.

Treat them all with a modicum of caution. You might feel there's no point in being nice to them as they won't be there for long . . . but they might take the same view.

If you do like them and do want to keep them happy, tell the boss-doctor how good they are. That way they'll get to come back.

GPs Proper (Proper GPs)

Am suddenly aware that, apart from that last bit, I am drifting into how-to-get-the-best-from-your-doctor-mode. Telling you stuff to aid your decision-making. Helping the patient! *Not* what this book is about. Maybe it's because we're rabbitting on about GPs, and maybe (just maybe) I don't really care whether they are happy or not.

I should really put that right. After all, they are the person you will have most contact with. No use having a great relationship with your hospital consultant if your GP refuses to do anything the consultant suggests (not likely, but it is the case that your GP continues to look after you and the consultant only advises).

So I really should make some effort.

We should start with a look at my earlier advice from earlier chapters. See if any of it doesn't pertain to GPs. So I checked with my GP guru ('return' appointment required . . . even longer wait).

Spouses, Family and Friends
. . . Apparently . . . GPs are less against accompanying persons. Can't understand this. Maybe it's so when they give you a ticking-off for not doing the things they told you last time, they have a witness that they did indeed tell you. We're not that bothered if you forget – we just tell you again. But they see you more often and want to change things, improve things. Your GP *wants* you to stop smoking. You're his family.

Know Your Enemy
They agree with *everything* I said about surgeons.

Students
GPs don't have enough time to teach students. They can only make time if that's 'their thing'. So

if the GP you see has a student with him, then education is his thing, not . . . making patients better . . .

Gifts
GPs hate gifts. Send them all anonymously to the hospital consultant whose name comes nearest to them in the alphabet.

Clothes
Their main concern is that you wear enough clothes to get home. Don't turn up in the middle of a blizzard in your pyjamas. It's not their fault you did that, but it's now their worry how to get you back.

Things Not to Do
Don't drip on the new carpet (neither rain nor blood). Hospital doctors don't care about the formica floors, but GPs *own* theirs.

Private medicine
Private GPs are a rarity in Scotland, but a bit more common down South. Treat them like your private stockbroker, not your butler. Don't forget you'll have to pay for all your drugs.

General General Practitioners Generally

Besides the above, there are things specific to GPs we haven't even thought about. Since they are simple folk, we'll keep the advice on how to deal with them similarly simple. Some straight-forward **'Do's and Don'ts'**. Of course, to approach the positives first would be entirely alien to the ethos of this book. As would having equal numbers.

Ten Don'ts

Don't *say 'while I'm here, Doctor . . .' unless you plan to follow up with '. . . I'll just clean the windows for you.'*
GPs run to a tight schedule. Theoretically, they want you to turn up with *one* problem, which they can deal with in the allotted time space. According to Bro., maybe one patient in a session will do this, the others dangling anything from two to seven diagnostic puzzles in front of increasingly tired eyes.

To be fair, this probably reflects an effort on the patient's part not to trouble the doctor with trifles. Thus we 'collect' a number of said trifles until it's worth turning up. All very commend-able, but plays havoc with the GP plan for four minutes per punter. Keep it to one problem; two at most. You don't make an appointment with the family solicitor, use the scheduled time completing all that Last Will and Testament farrago, then say 'while I'm here, there's one of my neighbours keeps chucking stuff over our garden hedge . . .'

★　　★　　★

Don't *insist on seeing the same doctor every visit.* Should really have touched on this whilst dealing with hospitals, where some patients like to insist on seeing the consultant. This is based on the assumption, occasionally false (he might be me!) that the consultant knows best. Even when this is true, seeing the same doctor every time runs the risk of his making the same mistake, missing the same diagnosis, every time. A fresh pair of eyes now and again does not go amiss.

The GP scenario introduces a further drawback. In hospitals, the consultant is the recognised boss, expert, the 'gold standard'. By the simple criterion of experience, he clearly holds sway. GPs, on the other hand, are theoretically of identical standing. If you persist in choosing the same one, how are the other guys going to feel?

. . . Unless, of course, you are a miserable heart-sink of a patient, whereupon seeing the same practitioner every time does keep five out of six doctors in your practice relatively happy.

Don't *take away the magazines in the waiting-room.* I don't really have to explain this one, do I?[3]

Don't *mention his overinflated salary.* I did touch on this with hospital consultants, but GPs can be even more touchy.

---

[3] Don't even, as a colleague admits when attending her own GP, cut out the recipes.

. . . Partly this is because the papers are always full of quotes on GP's 'average earnings' when this includes the hyper-commercial doctors scattered around the country with a finger in every pie (nice imagery . . .) or who look after celebrities, or the Queen, or Marks & Spencer's and basically earn the same as the Chairman. ('Top Docs' they'll call 'em. Never go see one if you actually have anything wrong with you.) It's like the average age of a class including the teacher and their assistant.

. . . But mainly because their salaries now depend on jumping through so many hoops that we punters don't know about. I first became aware of this a couple of years back, after giving a group of GPs a riveting talk on fibromyalgia. It had been recent talk of the steamie that they were all being paid £200 just for turning up and listening (. . . I heard that! . . .), and I made a light-hearted comment on this. It was explained that £2,000 had been docked from their previous salary figure, and to get this back they had to attend at least ten such lectures in a year. Hence this was interpreted to the world as their being paid £200 for every . . .

Don't *say 'you've* **got** *to do something'*
Apparently this rankles hugely with GPs. Maybe it's because they're the ones that spent five years at Med School followed by 20 years seeing patients and deciding when to do something . . . so being *ordered* to do something seems an assault on

their autonomy; immediately not helping the old doctor-patient relationship, and from your own point-of-view, not necessarily helping your health. Let's look at the possibilities.

a) Doctor was going to do something anyway, and still does so, but feels less good about it.
b) Doctor was going to do something anyway, but is so discomfited by the unwelcome pressure that he decides against it.
c) Doctor was not going to do anything (all that five-and-twenty years' experience and stuff suggesting he shouldn't), and sticks to his guns – leading to bad feeling, arguments or worse.
d) Doctor was planning not to do anything (all that . . .), but succumbs to pressure and does something he feels he shouldn't. Again with the possibilities of bad feelings etc.

Only in d) can you possibly gain, and only when the doctor was wrong in the first instance and your diagnostic prowess was superior. Now, this may well happen, but it's more likely your doctor will find himself prescribing unnecessary antibiotics, unnecessary painkillers (such as opiates) or requesting unnecessary investigations or hospital admissions. Since these are all against 'his better judgement', they will often be fruitless and this will modify his approach and judgement skills in dealing with you in the future. Not always to your advantage.

Oh, another thing. Why I particularly agree with this GP '**Don't**' piece of advice. One option to 'do something' is to send you to *me* for an opinion.

Don't *demand immediate detox because you've decided to stop drinking.*
I didn't realise this happened to GPs, but it overlaps with hospital experience. In the past, 'alcoholic' patients would be admitted because chronic intake had eventually made them very ill, or an acute binge had done the same, or they'd had to stop drinking a few days earlier and had drifted into the 'DTs' (*delirium tremens*). Nowadays they bounce through Accident & Emergency with a 'diagnosis of DTs' at three o'clock in the afternoon having given up drinking at lunchtime. They're not in DTs, but 'plan to stop drinking' and have come into hospital *just in case* they get the DTs. Currently, they're fine (if a bit drunk). To be honest, you could make a case that this is fair enough, but when they tell you they only stopped drinking because they ran out of vodka and the shops were shut . . .

Have suddenly realised what a limited-audience tip this is. How many readers out there does this refer to? But they do say the problem is increasing, and it was number six in Mal's list of eighteen thousand and twelve.

★   ★   ★

Don't *say 'my lawyer says you have to . . .'*
This is an extrapolation of the universal (surely?) raised-hackle response when anyone tells you 'ye huvtae'. Hackles are further raised if the huvtae-er is someone you hold in ill-regard – which will always include lawyers. The saving grace for the doctor here is that for once he has the moral high-ground. Medical reports, certificates and the like are legal documents. He has to take care over them, and signs them 'on soul and conscience' asserting them to be true in every respect. If he is being pressurised or hurried in any way, he is clearly justified in taking umbrage.

Whilst this will bring him a brief whiff of happiness, it is counter-productive to yourself. Better to await his offer of help – perhaps nudging him in that direction as you recount your problems – rather than commanding him by the authority of some unseen legal impresario (whom he knows he'll have to chase all year for his fee).

Don't *say 'I've waited three weeks for this appointment' when that's not true.*
The practice will almost certainly have records that show exactly when you made the appointment. The underlying advice, of course, is that you shouldn't lie about anything when it comes to discussing things with your GP. Cigarettes, alcohol, drugs, sexual encounters, bank balance . . . (sorry, slipped into Private Hospital mode for a second there . . .)

★   ★   ★

Don't *say . . .*
  'this can't be arthritis, it's too sore.'
  'I'm going to kill myself if you don't . . .'
  'you don't care . . . what do you know about suffering?'

Don't *demand he refer you to a hospital specialist.*
. . . erm . . . might not actually be one of Mal's . . .

Five Dos

Do *tell the truth, even if you think it sounds stupid.*
Usually it's the other stuff that's stupid.

Do *change to another practice if you think your GP is rubbish or if you really don't get on.*
Presumably either a) you're right, or b) you yourself are a bit . . . tricky.
  It's probably a).
  Either way, best all round if you arrange to be looked after by someone else. And it's a lot easier for everyone if *you* do this rather than have the GP 'delete' you from their list.
  And if you find your next GP is also rubbish and you don't get on, *then* you might give b) a little more consideration.

Do *let the practice know if you can't make an appointment.*
It helps them plan doughnut requirements for coffee breaks.

★　　★　　★

Do *leave your GP pots of money in your will.* Traditionally more normal than for hospital doctors, and easier for your GP to simply accept with good grace[4] (hospital doctors find it more awkward, ending up refusing or putting it into some complicated endowment fund for research).

It will help keep your doctor happy, whilst finally putting one over on your pesky offspring.

Do *observe this double-**Don't** tip (positive spin, eh?)* Rookie Mistake 1

Don't *walk three-quarters of a mile to the surgery, bringing a form for the GP to sign which states you can only walk ten yards.*

Not-quite-so-Rookie Mistake 1
Don't *ask for a house-call so that the GP can sign a form which states you can only walk ten yards . . . then stroll past his traffic-jammed Fiesta on your way to the bookies.*

And, just to finish off, a couple of linked pairs.

Do *'have a nice Christmas'* – he really means it.
Don't *'have a nice day'* – that's sarcasm.

---

[4] Though apparently he will have to pay tax and super-annuation.

Do *ask for a house-call because . . .*
  . . . you are unwell or housebound
  . . . you need diagnosed and stabilised before possible admission to hospital.

Don't *ask for a house-call because . . .*
  . . . it's raining
  . . . you are waiting for the gasman
  . . . you can't get an appointment at the surgery until tomorrow
  . . . you need a prescription
  . . . there's a good film on (particularly if you continue to watch it)

or, my personal favourite

  . . . 'my house is on your way home anyway.'

Hmmmmm . . .

. . . HOUSE CALLS

I suddenly realise just how important the house-call is. The big difference between GP-land and Hospital-land ('domiciliary visits' by consultants now being so rare). The need for house-calls in the first place is a big issue for GPs (you need to be proper-sick and proper-not-able to get out of the house. And it's not necessary just because you're a child . . . it's *easier* for you to get to the surgery – you just get carried). Once the house-call is in motion, it's worth a whole set of Dos and Dont's of its own.

Do be there at the time he turns up (particularly bad to be out playing football)
Do keep any pesky dogs well out of harm's way (preferably locked up in another room)
Do keep any pesky kids out of harm's way (preferably . . .)
Do put the TV off
Do have a nice warm room which is comfortable for you to be seen in (not the one where you locked the rabid dog)
Do be understanding if he keeps glancing at his Mercedes through the window (you might send little Jimmy out to 'watch it' – as long as he doesn't overcharge)
Do, if you're laid up in bed, plan some way to let him in . . . including . . .
Do, if you have some coded combination-lock entrance, let him know the number
Do always keep a thermometer, spatula, stethoscope and ophthalmoscope by your bed in case he forgets his bag.

And

Don't smoke, even though it is your own house
Don't offer him tea and cake, unless you are a good baker, whereupon offer him two.

Don't play music unless it's Beethoven or Radiohead

Don't sit with your laptop, Googling everything he says

Don't do anything else (talk on phone, text, have a shower, make dinner . . .)

Don't assume he can supply you with prescriptions and lines and all the other routine stuff he deals with at the surgery, but not at an *emergency* call-out

Don't think for a moment he'll be able to carry out anything resembling a full examination because 'your mother's there and she'll do as a chaperone'. Chaperones are for his benefit too.

OTHER PATIENTS

A big pile of **Dos** (See? Positive again.)

Do *always scowl at them in the waiting-room. If they are ahead of you in the queue, make it clear you are not aware of (or don't care about) this, and might at any time nip in front of them. If they are behind you in the queue, make it clear that you suspect them of planning this very manoeuvre, and would **not** be pleased.*

Take more space up on the bench/chairs than you have to.

Monopolise today's paper, or the only magazine that was printed this century.

Sniffle.

Cough
Sneeze.

Surrounded by that sort of behaviour in the waiting-room, the patient's going to think the GP is *such* a nice guy.

GLOSSARY[1]

S ome terms may have different meanings to doctors from what they mean to humans. So to avoid misunderstandings . . .

Acute: *see chronic*[2]
Angina: pain (normally) in the chest occurring (normally) with exercise and (normally) caused by narrowing of the arteries supplying the heart muscle. It is NOT:

a) breathlessness occurring with said exercise
b) chest pain occurring without said exercise (normally)

The surfeit of *normallys* is explained by my adherence to an old medical dictum that there

---

[1] Please note this is genuine attempt to help. Do not expect same level of entertaining unfriendly banter as elsewhere in book.
[2] Don't you just hate that? Just to save me writing it out twice. Lazy.

are no *alwayses* in medicine. Nothing is ever that certain or uncertain. Never.

Auscultation: listening to your heart or lungs with a stethoscope.

Blood Group: different proteins are present on the surfaces of red blood cells in different groups of people – such that other people's immune systems 'not used to' seeing these proteins will react to them.

We'll deal with the most well-known (and most important) – the ABO system. From each parent you can inherit the A protein (A), or the B protein (B), or neither (O). Adding up your inheritance from both patients (assuming you're not cloned) you can get AA, AB, AO, BB, BO or OO. Since the 'no proteins' gene doesn't negate the proteins from the other parent, AO and BO will make you type A and B respectively. So blood types can be A [AA or AO], B [BB or BO], AB [AB] or O [OO].

If you've got these proteins on your red cells, your body will 'get used' to them and NOT make antibodies to 'kill them' – but you will make anti-bodies to the other proteins. So, if you are 'Type A', you won't make antibodies to A proteins (otherwise your immune system would be really stupid), but you will make them to B proteins – so if somebody gives you B blood (or AB blood which has both proteins), you'll make antibodies and kill the new cells ('haemolysis') and get sick. But you'll be OK if given A blood. You'll also be OK with O [OO] blood, because there are no proteins on the cells to make antibodies to. That's why you can give O-blood to anybody (if Rhesus-ve; see below) – but people with O-blood can't get anything else as they'll make antibodies to everything, A or B. People with AB blood can get any of them as they won't make antibodies to anything – assuming they're Rhesus positive . . .

All right . . . I suppose I'd better do 'Rhesus' – another, entirely separate protein. You've either got it on your cells [positive] or you don't [negative]. If you've got it, you won't make antibodies to it so you can get Rh positive blood (or RH negative as it has no proteins). If you don't have it, you'll make antibodies, so you can *only* get Rh negative.

Putting these two systems together, you can give O Rh negative blood to anybody . . . unless they're incompatible by any of the hundreds of less 'Important' proteins – which is why blood is properly 'matched' with a sample of the recipient – put together and tested for any reaction – before given. Simple correct-group blood is only used in dire emergencies.

And the misconception? A special test is needed to identify blood grouping, and every other blood test under the sun ordered by the doctor to find out what's wrong with you will *not* tell either of you your Blood Group, so don't assume it will. I also view it as confused thinking when people giving blood want to brag they have the rarest blood group. That means they have the chance to help the *fewest* number of people. Maybe it's 'living on the edge' type of bragging, since if *they* have an accident in the future . . .

Blue Blood will often panic patients when they are having a sample taken. Blood directly from your *vein* is actually expected to look quite blue, no matter your ancestry. It's on its way to your lungs to get more oxygen, after losing it all to feed the tissues. First the blood goes to the right side of the heart which gives it a short pump into the lungs, gets tanked up with O2 which makes it red, then goes back to the left side of the heart which is stronger and can pump it right around the body. Blood in the peripheral *arteries* on the way to the tissues is therefore red. So if the blood the doctor takes *is* bright red . . . make sure you press on the hole that good bit longer afterwards . . .[3]

Cardiac Arrest is an acute emergency. The main chamber of the heart – the left ventricle – either stops beating all together (asystole) or trembles uselessly (ventricular fibrillation). Either way this pushes no blood at all around the body . . . which leaves the brain with about four minutes of back-up nutrients before it packs in for good. This is the time when the 'crash team' crash around

---

[3] Sometimes we deliberately take blood from an artery – to check oxygen levels. This is usually done at the radial artery at the wrist and is the NIPPIEST THING IN THE WORLD. The hole takes longer to heal because of the pressure in the artery, so you have to press for five full minutes or end up with a big throbby swelling.

you, trying to kick-start your heart either with a punch (honest), forceful massage (which has the added bonus of pushing some blood around the body) or an electrical jolt ('CLEAR!'). If you're going to have a cardiac arrest, I suggest you have it in Chicago's County General Hospital, since the success-rate in ER is at least five times as good as any other hospital on the planet.

Cardiac arrest is NOT 'heart failure', nor a 'heart attack' – though there are links.

Cartilage is stuff that lines the surfaces of bones where they meet each other in joints (articular cartilage). It's difficult to describe – a wet, spongy-yet-slidey gristle that can help shock-absorb by exuding fluid.[4] It doesn't show up on X-Ray, so 'wear-and-tear' arthritis can sometimes be diagnosed because the blank space on XR between the bone-ends becomes smaller as the cartilage is eroded ('loss of joint space').

The 'cartilages' you get damaged while badly twisting your knee, almost invariably it seems when playing football (the clue is you immediately had to stop playing) are not made of cartilage. They're hard half-moons of fibrous tissue (so proper names = menisci) which help the slightly unsuited shapes of the bones to fit better.

Chronic: See 'Acute'.

Dai: Welsh name, short for David. OK, not a frequent

---

[4] I assume this makes perfect sense to any students of hydraulics out there?

misapprehension, but gives me a chance to tell true story of when I was a registrar. My consultant was finishing his stint in 'general medicine' and was going round the ward to see which of his patients had problems in his own specialty and he should therefore keep, and which should be transferred to Dai Jones (surname changed to protect the here-at-least innocent), who was taking over the ward. He thought for some time at the foot of the bed of one borderline unfortunate, before finally announcing, *'I think we'll leave this patient to Dai . . .'*[5]

Dermatitis: just means inflammation of the skin. There are lots of different types. Eczema is a form of dermatitis ('atopic dermatitis'). The word neither suggests that your skin is dirty nor that the whole thing must have been caused by something at work (despite 'industrial dermatitis' being a very popular sub-form of contact dermatitis in the 70s).

Embolus: Usually some small something which breaks away and lodges in an artery or equivalent, blocking the blood supply to what maybe an important organ. Thus clots in the leg can break away and lodge in the lung (pulmonary embolus), or small clots forming in the heart can be sent

---

[5] When telling this story at Dai's retiral I painted myself as a conciliatory hero, hastening to the side of terrified patient. *It's all right, Sir, our other consultant's called Dai Jones, and he simply means we're getting Dai Jones to look after you.* His eyes opened a bit wider, his hands trembled a bit faster . . . *'I know! . . .'*

on their way to lodge in the brain and cause an embolic stroke. If you followed that whole double-circulation through the heart explanation (**Blue Blood** qv.), you'll see how clots in the leg cannot get to the brain because they get stuck in the lungs (unless there's a hole-in-the-heart which we won't go into right now . . .)

Doesn't have to be blood clots. You can get fat-emboli (following major bone fractures, the fat is from the marrow) or emboli of infected tissue ('mycotic').

You'll have spotted the plural of 'embolus' is 'emboli' (*em-bol-aye*).

Fracture: medical word for a broken bone. It is not something slightly less serious than a broken bone ('just a fracture'); it *is* a broken bone. The 'hairline fracture' does have some sugges-tion of less-seriousness (as long as that's not *at* the hairline), but since it essentially describes the difficulty seeing the fracture on X-Ray, it doesn't necessarily mean good news.

Conversely, I should clarify that finding a fracture is not always bad news. With a choice of other injuries – such as serious ligament damage – the frac-ture is often the one with the more straightforward management, healing, and longterm prospects.

Goitre: is a swelling of the thyroid gland in the neck. The gland can be 'overactive' or 'underac-tive'. When I was young, the associated thyroid eye disease was so commonly included in any demonstration pictures that everybody I knew thought 'goitre' described those big googly eyes. This is when I was 'young' . . . but studying medicine. I've always assumed people out there make the same mistake, and otherwise this paragraph is such a waste of space . . .

Glands: are organs in the body that produce useful stuff of some sort. The *endocrine* glands make hormones which they secrete directly into the blood – such as insulin from the pancreas, or thyroid hormone from the guess-where. Meantime the *exocrine* glands produce fluid for some local function – like the salivary glands to make your food all slippery and swallowable, or the prostate gland which does . . . a similar sort of thing.

'Lymph Glands' are not glands at all. They don't produce stuff. They are properly called 'lymph nodes', and are sophisticated filters of any material – including infective or even tumorous – which is being drained from a part of the body by the lymphatic system (a loosely-formed network of microscopic drainage channels which eventually drain all of the excess fluid stuff in the tissues [like the oedema of swollen ankles] back into the bloodstream). The lymph nodes have some infection-fighting cells in them, but these are often overrun and the node swells up – e.g. the nodes under your armpit when you have a boil on your arm. Patients have come to call them 'glands' because the effect is similar to the swelling of the salivary glands, such as the parotid, when you get viral infections such as Mumps attacking the salivary glands themselves.

As mentioned elsewhere, over the years doctors have also come to call them glands, making a creative use of inaccuracy to avoid confusion!

If it helps, remember mumps causes your glands to swell, and glandular fever doesn't (. . . didn't think it would).

Heart Attack: called a myocardial infarction ('MI') by doctors (or 'infarct'). This is when one of the narrow blood vessels supplying the heart muscle (coronary arteries) becomes blocked and the area of heart muscle supplied by that artery doesn't get its blood supply. If it's only for a short time, or the artery is only narrowed, then you might just get cramping pain in the heart muscle (angina) – just like the pain in the calf muscles if you overdo things. If for too long, the muscle fibres actually die from the lack of blood-borne oxygen (ischaemia), and you have an infarction. Depending on how much, and what part of the heart wall is damaged, you may then have failure of the heart as a pump, or damage to the heart's conduction mechanisms, leading to inefficient heart rhythms or even cardiac arrest.

Heart attack is NOT synonymous with either cardiac arrest or heart failure, but either can occur as a consequence of the heart attack.

Heart Failure: failure of the heart as a pump leading to ankle swelling and/or breathlessness depending how much the right and left sides of the heart are affected respectively. This can occur acutely (e.g. after a heart attack) or more

215

chronically (e.g. with hypertension or coronary heart disease). It can be severe and indeed life-threatening, but it is NOT the sudden stopping of the heart which = *cardiac arrest*.

Homoeopathy: (qv) is a *specific* alternative approach to therapy where vanishingly small quantities of a substance which would *produce* your symptoms are used to *cure* them. It is not synonymous with Alternative Medicine, of which it is but one branch.

Hypertension: higher-than-normal blood pressure. Not usually a short-term worry (unless hugely raised) but increases long-term possibilities of e.g. stroke or heart disease. *Doesn't* make you tense, or (usually) cause headaches.

Inflammation: is the response of an area of the body to various insults. Blood vessels become dilated and 'white cells' leak from the vessels and invade the tissues. This causes the classic (as in classic Latin) signs of '*rubor, calor et dolor*' (redness, heat and pain) where you can see it, such as in a joint or the skin. It can, of course, also cause more subtle episodes in various organs etc. inside the body (-*itis* means 'inflammation of' so it's all those *itises* we'll talk about elsewhere like hepatitis, pancreatitis etc.).

Whilst infection is a possible cause (e.g. abscess), the terms infection and inflammation are not synonymous. Rheumatoid arthritis has inflamed joints, but they are not infected. Medics need to be careful when telling someone they have 'inflammation' that the patient doesn't interpret this as infection. They pass this diagnosis of infection onto the next doctor they see who immediately assumes the first one is an idiot.

Instep: the bit on the top of the front of the foot. NOT the inside of the foot ('medial' aspect). To be honest, this isn't medical knowledge but football *nous*. The instep is the part of the foot that you hit a proper penalty with. Never take a penalty with the inside of the foot (you know the one; side-footed with the right foot towards the goalkeeper's left) since if the goalie guesses correctly he has a fair chance of stopping it. Whereas, even if he does guess correctly, the penalty drilled with the instep will go past, off, or even through him into the net. The corollary of this for goalies is that if you must dive at a penalty[6], go towards the potential stupid side-foot shot as you might just save that.

Lymphatics: see 'Glands'.

---

[6] Of course the actual best plan is to stay upright in the middle of the goals as that way you save all fluffed shots, quirky chips, some imperfectly hit proper shots, some side-footers once you spot where they're going, plus the occasional one blasted at you. This is 'best' if you want the best chance to save it. But goalies don't do this – for two reasons. One is that the well-blasted shot might take their head off. But more important than a head is street-cred. If you stand in the middle and a fluffish shot does go past you, you look a right toffee; whereas if you dive and the ball dribbles into the centre of the net, you were 'sent the wrong way'. Almost all goalies put their reputation in front of their team's chances of winning the match. [World Cup 2006. England v Portugal. 'Nuff said.]

217

Numb: no feeling *at all*. Not fuzzy/tingling/pins-and-needley. None. It's like when the dentist gives you a jag *after* you've waited for it to work properly – such that he can drill huge holes in your nerve-endings and you feel *nothing* – that's numb. When it's just starting to work, and later when it's coming back towards normal and feels odd/fuzzy (just before it gets sore again), that isn't numb.

The medical terms are reasonably precise and go back to the old Greeks again. Numb is *anaesthesia* – the Greek prefix *a* or *an* meaning without, no, lack of (as in *anaemia* – lack of blood; *amoral* – lack of morals; and, of course, *abetalipoproteinaemia*). So no feeling at all. Literally, no sensation. None of the five. So a general anaesthetic leaves you with no feelings, no touch, no taste, no hearing etc (mind you, anaemia isn't *no* blood). Pins-and-needles, or the sensation you get at the dentist's as it comes back is *paraesthesia* (*para*: beyond [paranormal] or alongside [paraolympics]) – a sensation that's a bit different from normal. If it's clearly unpleasant, it's *dysaesthesia*.

Nurse: NOT an altruistic caring angel sent from Heaven as the patient's only protection against the evil doctors. As demonstrated elsewhere, it's the other way round.[7]

Pain-killers: 'analgesics' in doctor parlance, do exactly what they say on the tin. They kill pain.

---

[7] Apologies for the ambiguity. Not suggesting nurses are sent to protect doctors from the evil patient.

Mainly by killing the appreciation of pain (not that many of us appreciate it much) via their actions on the brain. In increasing order of 'strength' (and toxicity) they include things like paracetamol, codeine, dihydrocodeine, tramadol and the 'proper' opiates like oxycodone, morphine and diamorphine (*heroin*, or *smack*, as your mother calls it). A totally separate group of drugs is the *anti-inflammatories* – usually termed 'NSAIDs' (Non-Steroidal-Anti-Inflammatories). Drugs like ibuprofen (Brufen, Neurofen), diclofenac (Voltarol), naproxen (Naprosyn) and etoricoxib (Arcoxia) are also true to their tin-blurbs and reduce inflammation e.g. in joints and muscles, lessening pain that way (mainly). Most doctors are aware that some patients who say they are taking 'just painkillers' are actually on anti-inflammatories – such as Brufen – with all their inherent tummy-problems, but you might as well also know about the distinction.

Pull, Strain, Sprain: all of these are the same thing. We usually use *pull* or *strain* with muscles, *strain* or *sprain* with ligaments. None is automatically more serious than any of the others. They describe a tear of some fibres, with a small amount of irritative bleeding around it. These are tiny 'microscopic' fibres – so it's not a 'tear' in the sense of a 'torn' muscle.

Muscles move limbs by contracting and pulling things towards each other. A strain occurs when it overdoes such a contraction, or pulls at the wrong time (e.g. whilst being stretched by some-thing else) or when it's stiff or cold. Ligaments are thin, slightly elastic membranes that sit positioned around joints so that the joints don't move too far out of place. They are strained by sudden surprise movements in joints, such as going over on your ankle, or being tackled by an exuberant/vicious midfielder.

Either damaged area is painful when you stretch it, but gradually settles as a small scar of fibrous tissue forms. This is never quite as strong as the original tissue. Standard sports-medicine-think suggests we should gently stretch the affected area during the days immediately after the injury, while the scar is producing itself, so that it forms to some extent in the force lines of the muscle, making it that bit stronger than a mish-mash of scar tissue that'll burst the first time you try to run for a bus or reach for a pint.

Rheumatics / Rheumatism: both layman terms with no specific medical meaning (though in the old days *rheumatism* referred to proper arthritis). So the question 'is it rheumatism or just rheu-matics, Doctor?' doesn't mean anything. Arthritis, on the other hand (or even the same one) is inflam-mation of the joints. '-*itis*' means 'inflammation of' apparently from the Ancient Greek (through 'Modern Latin' – whatever that is), though since the Ancient Greeks had no idea what inflamma-tion was, I've never quite followed. Anyways, this single piece of etymological knowledge explains lots of inflammation-of words such as *hepatitis* (liver), *gingivitis* (gums), *tendonitis* (also written as *tendinitis* for some reason) and *cellulitis* (skin), as well as giving us the apparently impossible word for inflammation of the ilium – *iliitis*. 'Fibrositis' would suggest inflammation of the fibrous tissue, but we're not convinced this actually exists and the word is an invention of slightly-less-Ancient GPs to explain inexplicable pains.

Note that 'arthritis' means that there is inflammation in the joint, not just pain (arthralgia).

Scan: there are lots of different scans. MRI scans, CT scans, UltraSound scans . . . Most doctors when saying 'a scan' with no qualifying term to another doctor used to mean an Isotope Scan, though with the progress of technology we have recently been moving towards the default position being a CT scan. An Isotope scan is when a substance labelled with a radioactive isotope is injected into the patient and the body-scanning gamma-camera shows where the substance goes to, giving 'hot' and 'cold' spots. They may show inflammation (e.g. in a bone scan) or show up a particular organ. A particularly neat example of the latter is a thyroid scan. An isotope of Iodine is used (^{121}I for the nuclear physicists among you) and the thyroid sucks this up from the blood because it uses iodine to make thyroid hormone or thyroxine ($C_6H_2I_2OH\text{-}O\text{-}C_6H_2I_2\text{-}C_2H_3NH_2COOH$ for the nuclear chemists among you – can't say this book isn't casting a wide net . . .).

So you get a perfect picture of the thyroid tissue, and you can look for 'cold spots'.

A CT or CAT (Computerised Axial Tomography) scan is essentially a repeated X-Ray taken from lots of different angles (that's why your body is enveloped in that mini-car-wash thing). The computer puts all the images together and comes up with a slice-by-slice representation of the relevant part of the body. It's usually got quite a high X-Ray exposure.

An MRI scan (Magnetic Resonance Imaging) doesn't use X-Rays. It rather impressively detects changes in electron spin in magnetic fields and since all the different tissues in the body behave slightly differently (much to do with water content) this gives a more precise slice-by-slice representation of the area than even the CT scan. As it puts your body inside a giant magnetic field, pieces of potentially magnetic material can actually move unpredictably – so you DON'T get one done if you've got a metal clip in your brain (and we don't use it to identify slivers in your eyeball after a welding accident). And it's not just bits of metal inside you. This magnetic field is immensely powerful – apparently being able to toss an errant drip-stand across the room. The MRI scanner is recognised as the one that makes a noise like a sinking Titanic, and is even more claustrophobic than the CT scanner.

An Ultrasound scan is the one with the jelly and the metal 'probe' moved gently over your skin. We think Ultrasound waves (essentially very very high frequency sound – say, above what a dog can hear and add six) are pretty safe. It's been used for many years for looking at babies in the womb[8] – indeed right from the time of its invention, which nowadays seems a bit cavalier – and has had very few problems. The pictures are less precise than the two modalities above. Indeed to us normal doctors they look like a demonstration of the famous 124 different types of . . . er . . . Inuit snow. But Ulstrasound scans are quick, cheap, and use – we hope – no potentially toxic rays.

Simple X-Rays we *never* call scans. We will thus get confused if you talk about having had a scan that was actually an Xray.

I might cite the above to explain why, if you ask the doctor what the scan you had yesterday showed, he always looks like he has no idea what you're talking about. Clearly he will be uncertain which of the possible scans you refer to. In reality, there are lots of other reasons:

1 He'll have no idea who you are. Particularly if you accost him with the question as he's innocently walking along the corridor. He'll also be wondering whether or not you are *his* patient (or indeed anybody's patient – remind me next time to call the cops). You all look the same to us. His first manoeuvre will thus be to look for your name . . .

---

[8] Pioneered in my home town of Glasgow. One of the great three Scottish inventions, after television and before deep-fried Mars Bars . . . so about two in the morning.

on that funny bracelet-thing, or above your bed, where he's less concerned with your name than hopefully some *other* doctor's name sitting alongside it[9].

2 Once you are reluctantly identified as his patient, he'll have no idea what he ordered yesterday. We can't remember one patient's plans from another.

3 Once he knows which scan he ordered, he won't know whether the result is back.

And while he's going through all of the above, the ever-present fear in the back of his mind is that the scan in question may have shown up something not-very-nice and he is about to be sucked into an important and sad conversation for which neither participant is at all prepared.

To my mind, all of these hesitations are entirely reasonable (particularly not remembering which patient is which, my personal bête-noire) but doctors aren't trained to expect patients and relatives to be reasonable. They assume everybody goes for the media doctors-should-know-everything-otherwise-they're-crap approach. So he'll go all defensive and try to pretend he knows

[9] You're probably thinking it must be his patient, or they wouldn't ask. But no. Many patients will demand from random passing doctor 'when are you letting me home?' to which I've always replied 'I'm afraid it's not up to me, I'm not your doctor. He'll be around later.' Mainly because I can't decide between the two temptations: 'Oh – it'll be *weeks* yet . . .' or 'Today!!'

exactly what he's talking about from the start . . .
and . . . that's . . . when . . . you've . . . *got'im*:

Any word on my brother's scan?
Oh yes, your brother . . . he's . . . had his scan . . .
and we're just waiting for the result.
I thought the machine was broken?
*Well . . . yes, it was – **is**, I mean . . . I was thinking*
*of his previous scan. The . . . **other** . . . scan. We're*
waiting for this one to be done.
No. The machine that analyses the results was
broken. They did the scan yesterday.
Of course they did . . . true . . .we, I, don't really
think of the scan as done until the results are
analysed . . .
And you'll let me know soon-as?
Of course.
That's great. You're much more helpful than Doctor
McTavish.
Doctor McTavish? Doesn't he work at the Royal?
Yes. That's the hospital my brother's in.

Sensible Shoes: do not simply = flat shoes.
Sensible shoes are covered (avoiding snake bites
seems sensible to me), formed and supportive
around the heels. (Sandals are never sensible, no
matter what your wife or daughter tells you. You
have to do some funny thing with your feet and
the front-bit of your knees to stop sandals flying
off into the swimming pool every time you take
a step. This funny thing can't be good for you.)

They should also have thick skwudgy soles[10] that both support your feet and act as some shock-absorption for your knees and hips and back. The best shoes in the world are . . . TRAINERS (rheumatologists can't smell).

Flatness is over-rated. A big heel is indeed daft, but thin leather-soled brogues like what surgeons and lawyers wear to Rotary Club dinner-dances ruin your knees despite having no heel on them (as opposed to *in* them). Even if you don't dance. People can run twenty-six miles in a trainer (not that I'm suggesting for a moment that *that*'s a good idea). Try that in a surgeon's brogue, and your nominated charity will go out of business. Mind you, there could be an upside to this, and people will stop doing the crazy running-26-miles-for-charity in the first place. Why do they do that? Is it to justify doing something clearly stupid by saying it's for a good cause? Like white-water-rafting, or bungee-jumping, or letting someone lop out your perfectly healthy kidney just to help someone else (OK maybe a step too far), marathon running is totally senseless and also knacks your knees. What is the point? It's not as if these people are trying to *win*. Whenever a

[10] Unless you are really old, when over-skwudginess can stop ageing nerves telling your brain 'where your feet are' (remember proprioception?) whereupon you feel like you're walking on mushrooms made from cotton wool and fall over. Breaking one or more of your osteoporotic bones.

patient tells me they ran in the la-de-da marathon (or '*fun*-run') I always ask them if they won. When this meets with a confused look, I ask what position they came in – ready to answer their proud 'seven thousand and twelfth' with an encouraging 'ooh that doesn't sound very good' and 'still, better luck next time'. At which point they tell me it was for charity and that's supposed to make it sensible. Why? If you go round all your pals asking for £10 for Cancer-Relief, they'll give it to you. For them to refuse unless you give yourself osteoarthritis or smack your head against a tree whilst white-water-rafting would surely seem churlish.

Shock: is a hugely dangerous situation in a seriously ill patient whose blood pressure falls, heart struggles, kidney fails ('when the Staphylococcal infection spread to his bloodstream, the patient went into septicaemic shock') and is NOT something you suffer after some bad news ('following the penalty decision, the entire team was in shock').

Steroids: as usually prescribed by doctors are *corticosteroids*. These are powerful anti-inflammatories and suppressors of the immune system used therefore in such diseases as asthma and arthritis. They are not *anabolic steroids*, and will not give you big shoulders, a hairy chest or make you run 100 metres in 9.2 seconds. (Actually, they may cause a touch of one of these because of overlapping effects. I'll leave any female advocates of Murphy's Law among you to guess which.).

It's worth knowing that steroids are substances we have naturally in the body, made by the adrenal glands. Prescribed steroids are extra or more powerful[11], and if we're on them for some time, our adrenals 'forget' how to make the natural ones. Since they are necessary to maintain blood pressure, help organs such as the heart respond to stress etc, it's very important NEVER TO STOP THEM SUDD-.

This won't make just your doctor very unhappy.

Stroke: a neurological (brain etc.) occurrence that can be due to a small clot, or bleed, or other causes. Classically it consists of weakness or other problems on one side (or part of one side) of the body. Speech can be affected in different ways. The muscles of speech may be weak or unco-ordinated leading simply to poor enunciation (dysarthria), or the brain itself may not put things together correctly, producing a more complex difficulty with constructing sentences or word-finding (dysphasia). The likelihood of speech problems with stroke depends on which

[11] Cortisol (hydrocortisone) is the main steroid in the body. We make about 30mg per day. Replacement therapy for someone whose adrenals make none is thus 30mg. The most common steroid tablet is prednisolone, about four times as potent. So 7.5mg prednisolone = 30mg cortisol. Perhaps because of this, side-effects with prednisolone seem less troublesome if your dosage is below 7.5mg.

side of the brain is involved. The left side of the brain works the right side of the body (I was going to say 'and vice-versa', but that's unnecessary since clearly if the brain's right side also worked the right side of the body that would be incredibly pointless, and you'd keep falling over. So I've saved some time by missing it out). In almost all right-handed people, the speech centres are in the left (dominant) hemisphere of the brain. With left-handers it's about fifty-fifty. So most people with the 'dysphasia' speech problems after a stroke will have any accompanying weakness on the right.

Stroke is NOT another word for a heart attack (and nor is *shock*).

Surgeons: Totally reasonable, hard-working men and women to whom I give a harder time than they deserve.

Tender: means sore *when you press it*. It is not a lesser pain than 'painful'.

Zog: 'Acute' is short-lasting, or sudden in onset. 'Chronic' is long-lasting. Neither chronic nor acute pain is by definition any more or less severe than 'painful'.

'Zog' is my word for this, unfortunately making it tricky for anyone searching for 'acute' and 'chronic' in, say, a glossary.

Top Top Tip
Treat your doctor as you would your garage mechanic . . . honest . . .

Leabharlanna Poibli Chathair Bhaile Átha Cliath
Dublin City Public Libraries